Beyond the Deal and Tyrone R. Johnson

"*Beyond the Deal* is a must-read for leaders navigating the post-private equity landscape. Drawing on twenty-five years of experience on both sides of the private equity table, Ty delivers actionable insights and a practical roadmap for driving value and long-term success."

–Jason Brown, PhD
Ernst & Young Faculty Fellow and Professor of Accounting,
Kelley School of Business, Indiana University

"Tyrone provides a roadmap for first time CEOs or owners selling their company to private equity. A must-read that provides a commonsensical approach to embracing and winning within the PE ownership structure."

–Scott Riggs
Chief Operating Officer, White Cap

"Tyrone has been on both sides of the private equity table, as a company operator and PE investor. This book focuses on the key things you need to get right as an operator, running a business to PE timescales and goals. Read it to set off in the right direction, stay the course, and ultimately win the prize of a high value exit."

–Jonathan Duck
CEO, Amtico Ltd

BEYOND THE DEAL

BEYOND THE DEAL

A CEO'S GUIDE TO PRIVATE EQUITY SUCCESS

TYRONE R. JOHNSON

Advantage | Books

Published by Advantage Books, Charleston, South Carolina.
An imprint of Advantage Media.

ADVANTAGE is a registered trademark, and the Advantage colophon is a trademark of Advantage Media Group, Inc.

Printed in the United States of America.

10 9 8 7 6 5 4 3 2 1

ISBN: 979-8-89188-364-2 (Paperback)
ISBN: 979-8-89188-365-9 (eBook)

Library of Congress Control Number: 2026900640

Cover design by Ruthie Wood.
Layout design by Matthew Morse.

This publication is designed to provide accurate and authoritative information in regard to the subject matter covered. It is sold with the understanding that the publisher is not engaged in rendering legal, accounting, or other professional services. If legal advice or other expert assistance is required, the services of a competent professional person should be sought.

Advantage Books is an imprint of Advantage Media Group. Advantage Media helps busy entrepreneurs, CEOs, and leaders write and publish a book to grow their business and become the authority in their field. Advantage authors comprise an exclusive community of industry professionals, idea-makers, and thought leaders. For more information go to **advantagemedia.com**.

02-03-2026 10:4

To my wife, Amy, and to my children, Tyler and Sydney.

Contents

About the Author

Tyrone (Ty) Johnson has a rich career as both a multi-time CEO and strategic private equity partner. In his twenty-five-year career, he has held various senior executive leadership roles across industrial, finance, technology, and other sectors. Currently, he leads Cascade Services—a premier residential tri-trade services platform he joined in 2022—as its CEO. For the past three years, he has successfully steered this enterprise's business and strategic development with the goal of being the optimal acquirer for family-owned business operators.

Before joining Cascade Services, Tyrone served as a leader in numerous reputable establishments, including as operating partner at Trive Capital (2020–2022), CEO at publicly traded Select Interior Concepts (2017–2020), CEO at Residential Design Services (2015–2017), and president (2015) and VP/general manager (2014) of OmniMax International Inc. He also served as the senior VP at Mannington Mills Inc. (2012–2013) and president of Amtico (2008–2012). For five years, up to 2008, Tyrone advanced as a leader in different divisions of Armstrong World Industries, from general manager of residential sales (2002–2003) to VP of strategic accounts (2003–2006) to VP and general manager (2006–2008). Tyrone began his career with GE Capital in 1994 and held various positions of increasing responsibility, culminating in the role of director of quality (Master Black Belt).

Tyrone attained his MBA from DePaul Driehaus in 2000 and his BBA in Marketing from Howard University in 1994.

Though his role in private equity keeps Tyrone very busy, he still finds time to invest in his community, his alma mater, and his passions—such as education, especially the arts and humanities. As such, he has served on the Board of Trustees of The Woodruff Arts Center since 2020 and on the Advisory Council of 21st Century Leaders since 2015.

Tyrone resides in Florida with his wife, Amy, and children, Tyler and Sydney.

Abbreviations and Acronyms

AI	Artificial intelligence
B2B	Business-to-business
B2C	Business-to-consumer
CRM	Customer relationship management
CAC	Customer acquisition cost
CLV	Customer lifetime value
CRR	Customer retention rate
DAU	Daily active users
EBITDA	Earnings before interest, taxes, depreciation, and amortization
ERP	Enterprise resource planning
EV	Enterprise value
FCF	Free cash flow
HR	Human resources
HVAC	Heating, ventilation, and air conditioning
IOI	Indication of interest
IRR	Internal rate of return
KPI	Key performance indicator
LOI	Letter of intent
MAU	Monthly active users
M&A	Mergers and acquisitions
MOIC	Multiple on invested capital
NPS	Net promoter scale
PE	Private equity

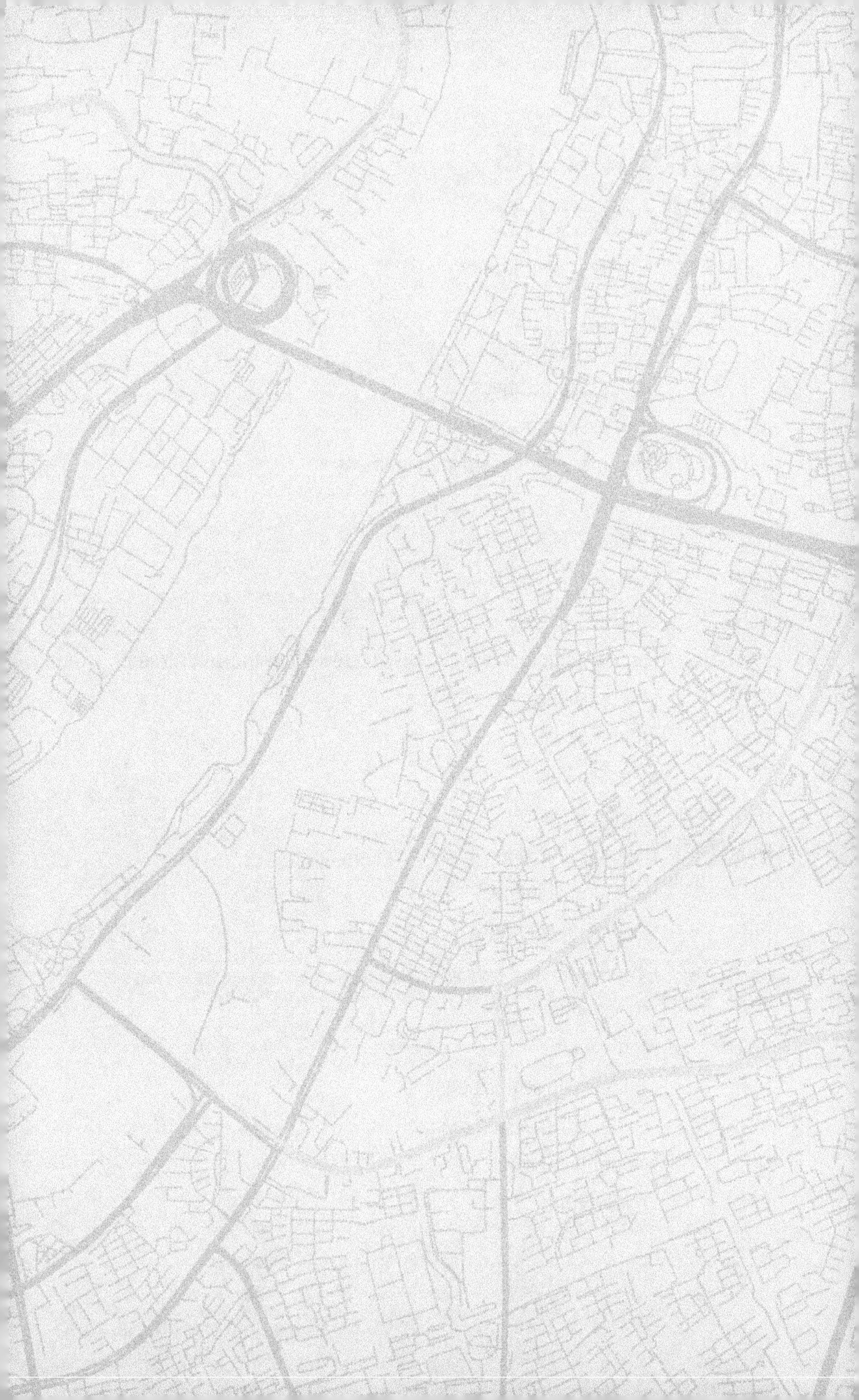

Acknowledgments

I extend my heartfelt gratitude to my friends, family, and colleagues (past and present) who have helped me grow into the business executive and private equity leader that I am today. Though the list of people I would like to acknowledge is inexhaustible, I would especially like to acknowledge Joe McDougall, partner at Trive Capital. Through our years of professional interaction and friendship, I have learned a great deal from Joe. He has been exceptionally gracious in sharing his wisdom, knowledge, and feedback on the development of my book. Not only did his input encourage me, but it also challenged me to go further and deeper in my debut publication. Thank you, Joe.

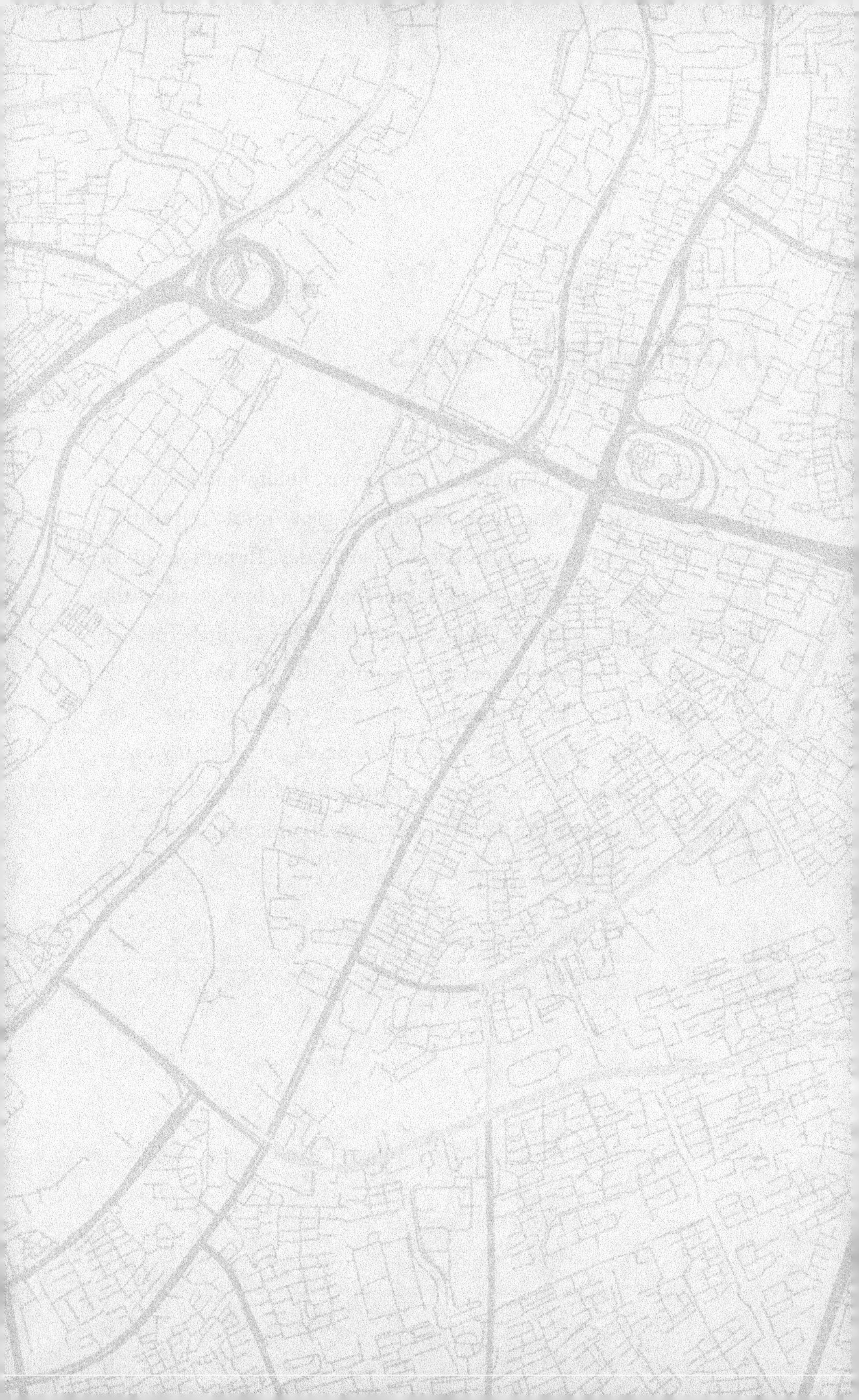

Introduction

After months or years of navigating the sales process, you are ready to take your business to the next level. You put in the work and managed to obtain private equity (PE). It was no easy feat. Congratulations!

At this juncture, what is the way forward?

You have shifted from limited capital for growth, insufficient operational expertise, leadership gaps, and possible debt management to fresh new challenges that come with this new ownership structure. You no longer have the final say and full autonomy. Investors are eager to see the business achieve rapid growth, causing you unprecedented stress. You need to figure out how to merge your business's culture with that of the investors to ensure this ship sails smoothly into uncharted waters.

The complete control over your schedule that you once enjoyed has changed. PE partners have needs, questions, data requests, and other expectations. Learning how to navigate these needs while staying laser-focused on the business is essential to your success and the success of the business. This is the time that you could have spent on operational improvements or customer development. If this wasn't enough, the staff who helped your business achieve its current success are concerned about the company's new direction. Will they jump ship? Instinct tells you to be concerned.

All along, you thought the hardest part was behind you once you closed the deal. However, reality says otherwise.

PE experts have found that nine out of ten founders and entrepreneurs who sell their businesses to PE firms really don't know what they're getting themselves into.[1] Sadly, that's one reality. It does not have to be yours.

Perhaps you are coming into this company as an executive who has never navigated a PE business before. The uncharted territory is extensive. You know you need some guidance if you are to achieve the desired results in record time.

With the average holding period being approximately five years,[2] the clock is ticking, and you are running out of time.

The goal of this book is to help you experience an alternative reality. That is the reality of one out of ten entrepreneurs, where you are fully prepared to level up using PE investment. Your goal as a nonfounding executive is to efficiently lead this business to realizing its full financial potential. Yes, this terrain is new and strange, but you know what you're doing.

Beyond the Deal is your battle plan.

Drawing from twenty-five years of executive experience across both sides of PE partnerships, this guide addresses the critical challenges most operators face. In addition, I have worked for nearly twenty years as a PE portfolio CEO and operating partner and have significant insider insights to share with you. My dual experience as both PE portfolio CEO and operating partner provides insights

---

1   Todd Sullivan, host, *The Wise Exit*, episode 37, "The Private Equity Playbook and How to Create Generational Wealth with Adam Coffey," May 31, 2023, Spotify, 12:51, https://open.spotify.com/episode/2coJBF6vOM8Du9PyJKKF9D.

2   James Chen, "Private Equity Explained with Examples and Ways to Invest," Investopedia, updated September 2, 2025, https://www.investopedia.com/terms/p/private-equity.asp.

from both sides of these partnerships, including practical insights for navigating the transition. Steering cultural shifts, analyzing and developing financial frameworks, team building, managing investor expectations, orchestrating mergers and acquisitions and integration successes, and implementing winning exit strategies are among my areas of expertise.

Through the pages of this book, my goal is to guide you after selling your business to PE or making the career shift to PE executive, demystify PE operations, prepare you for PE's expectations, and help you build trust as a founder or entrepreneur with your financiers.

We begin in chapter 1 by discussing the mindset common among PE partners and the mindset that is most ideal for your success. Some of the questions we answer are "What train of thought and understanding do you need as an operator (founder or corporate executive)?" and "What mindset does the investment team need to have for you to succeed?"

We then move on to discussing the myriad changes you will experience, the financial metrics you need to stay on top of, and the keys to integration. Your team may need to be upgraded. As such, we will look at how you can achieve that while advocating with your board. Then, we will discuss mergers and acquisitions change management, organic growth, preparations for selling the enterprise, and your options for your career after exiting the platform.

If you read this book, you will remove the guesswork and give yourself the peace of mind that puts the odds of success firmly in your favor. Business comes with ambiguities and anxieties, but navigating PE concerns doesn't have to be among them.

As with most matters, it's best to start at the beginning. We can all agree that every successful venture (and even action) begins with a thought. As such, what better place to start than to look at matters of your mind? In our first chapter, we will take a thoughtful look at alignment of your mindset with that of your investors and other business partners.

Let us proceed to our first chapter.

CHAPTER 1

ESSENTIAL MINDSET SHIFTS FOR PE SUCCESS

The man who focuses on contribution and who takes responsibility for results no matter how junior, is, in the most literal sense of the phrase, "top management." He holds himself accountable for the performance of the whole.[3]

—PETER DRUCKER

How you think directly influences how you execute in business. As such, to understand how to navigate the post-sale experience of transitioning away from entrepreneurship or—if you are joining—from a corporate role to a private equity (PE) position, it's important to start by looking at the ideal mindset to cultivate.

For our purposes, *mindset* can be defined as how you execute your responsibilities or work in the business. The most advantageous mindset you can have is one that focuses on answering this question: "How do I advance the agenda of the company and the PE investor?"

---

3   Peter F. Drucker, *The Effective Executive* (Butterworth-Heinemann, 1999).

Business is demanding, whether you are managing the platform company (a business purchasing other businesses) or add-ons (businesses acquired). A successful operator (i.e., founder, entrepreneur, or executive of a business that receives PE investment) requires a certain frame of mind when dealing with investors and operating partners. Operating partners also have their unique mindsets. They are individuals or organizations hired by the PE firm to provide tactical assistance when and where necessary. An operating partner could be any type of professional who has worked in the industry or a similar operation. If a PE firm determines that the business needs stronger financial leadership, marketing, human resources (HR), or an alternative specialization, the PE firm will elect to hire an individual to fill that gap. In some cases, it may opt to hire a generalist. In other cases, the operating partner may be on the board, or the CEO may need to report to them. Regardless of the context you find yourself in, you must figure out how to maintain your relationships with the operating partner and/or your investor.

When you close the sale on your business, or if you commanded a great deal of independence in your corporate role, it is no longer about you and your interests alone. You now must think about collaboration and shared vision more than or in alignment with a level of autonomy and self-determination.

CASE STUDY
Dan Glickberg and Fairway Market's PE Partnership

The dream of most entrepreneurs is to grow a thriving business that is not only profitable but also makes an impact. Nathan Glickberg accomplished that. He founded

Fairway Market in New York City in 1933.[4] With tenacity and drive, he took one gourmet grocery store and developed it into a chain of stores across New York. His son, Dan Glickberg, later took to the helm and continued his father's legacy.[5] In 2007, with continued growth, Fairway Market sold a controlling stake of the company to Sterling Investment Partners.[6] Sterling Investment Partners brought in $150 million in capital investment, facilitating further expansion of the enterprise. Four years later, the business managed to generate revenues of up to $550 million.[7]

Partnering with the PE firm wasn't without its challenges. The PE firm introduced changes to help the business improve performance. Sterling hired a new CEO and CFO, among other top professional management, thus introducing two key changes.[8] Then there was misalignment regarding the vision: Glickberg wanted to further the business's premium branding, while the PE firm expected to focus on a leaner but broader enterprise (fewer staff) with economy product offerings.[9]

---

4   "Why We're Like No Other Market," About Us, Fairway, accessed July 16, 2025, https://www.fairwaymarket.com/about-fairway/.

5   "About Dan," Dan Glickberg Food, accessed July 16, 2025, https://www.danglickbergfood.com/.

6   Sumathi Reddy, "Fairway Grocery Chain Targets an Expansion," *The Wall Street Journal*, July 11, 2011, https://www.wsj.com/articles/SB10001424052702304760604576427983426433672.

7   Ibid.

8   Noam Wasserman, *The Founder's Dilemmas: Anticipating and Avoiding the Pitfalls That Can Sink a Startup* (Princeton University Press, 2012).

9   Felix Barber and Michael Goold, "The Strategic Secret of Private Equity," *Harvard Business Review* 85, no. 9 (2007): 53–61.

Glickberg significantly misunderstood PE and how it works. The operational and financial scrutiny were new to him because of his lack of experience working in a PE environment. For instance, though the business had financial reporting, a higher standard of financial reporting was now required by the PE firm. Decisions that previously could be made by Glickberg alone now needed board approval.[10] Many founders would find these changes somewhat degrading and a blow to their ego as they struggle with a sense of diminished confidence, authority, and identity.

Likely because of this friction, Glickberg ultimately stepped down from leading his family-founded business shortly before the company's initial public offering in 2013.[11]

Unfortunately, after Fairway went public in 2013, due to aggressive expansion, the business's cumulative debts mushroomed to $270 million.[12] By 2016, the company's debt was at $300 million, and its only option was to file for bankruptcy.[13] The company then filed for bankruptcy again in 2020.[14]

---

10   Claudia Zeisberger, Michael Prahl, and Bowen White, *Private Equity in Action: Case Studies from Developed and Emerging Markets* (Wiley, 2017).

11   "Fairway Struggles in Public Spotlight," *Crain's New York Business*, March 17, 2014, https://www.crainsnewyork.com/article/20140317/HOSPITALITY_TOURISM/303169982/fairway-struggles-in-public-spotlight.

12   Eileen Appelbaum and Andrew W. Park, "How Private Equity Ruined a Beloved Grocery Chain," *The Atlantic*, February 16, 2020, https://www.theatlantic.com/ideas/archive/2020/02/how-private-equity-ruined-fairway/606625/.

13   Rosemary Batt and Eileen Appelbaum, "Private Equity Pillage: Grocery Stores and Workers at Risk," *The American Prospect*, October 26, 2018, https://prospect.org/2018/10/26/private-equity-pillage-grocery-stores-workers-risk/.

14   "Fairway Returns to Bankruptcy, Aims to Sell Manhattan Stores," *Bloomberg*, January 22, 2020, https://www.bloomberg.com/news/articles/2020-01-22/fairway-said-to-seek-bankruptcy-that-keeps-some-stores-open?embedded-checkout=true.

This story begs the questions: If the CEO and the PE firm had been aligned with a shared vision, would the trajectory of this business have remained the same? Would Glickberg have stayed at the helm to ensure that the business his father built rose to even higher heights while staying true to his desire for a premium offering?

Looking at the Fairway Market case study, you may note that there was a significant divide between the CEO and the PE firm's vision for the company. Let's look at the operator's mindset first and address what elements constitute the most beneficial mindset for operators to have.

Five Critical CEO Adaptations

Fairway Market built its four-decade reputation on quality goods and premium service. It was proud of its premium branding and managed to maintain it for close to forty years. The misalignment was not in wanting expansion, but in a mismatched expansion that did not hold true to these founding values. Without a shared vision and values, effective collaboration is impossible. These are elements of the right mindset for CEOs to have. Next, we'll look at these elements of the right mindset and more.

VALUES AND VISION ALIGNMENT

Misaligned expectations between operators and PE firms inevitably create friction. Therefore, when going into partnership with a PE firm, you must choose a firm that aligns with your company's values and vision. With that alignment comes the ease of doing business together as partners. It should never be just about the money that a

PE partnership can offer. It is not uncommon to find founders and CEOs in their new PE reality struggling because they did not learn how PE works or what changes they would encounter. One sure way of ensuring success is getting the right partner on the other side of the table in the first place. Success is almost guaranteed when your partner aligns with your vision and values.

GROUNDED

Operators who ultimately succeed in their PE partnerships are often exceptionally grounded. Their rootedness—mental and emotional stability as a default setting of their personalities—equips them to adapt to the new PE terrain. Healthy consideration of the self is not only helpful to live a productive life; it is vital. The problem is when it is inflated. This occurs when successful operators assume their proven methods will continue to work and enter the PE world with the belief that the rules that have helped them rise to this new level are the same ones that will help them succeed going forward.

Many successful operators are unique individuals with exceptional and admirable confidence and proactive drive. What is peculiar about some of them is the air of *bravado*—albeit not arrogance—that they possess.

Some CEOs I've worked with even believe they possess a type of magic or "secret sauce." Unfortunately, that perspective is false. The entrepreneurial playbook that elevated you to your present success will not sustain you in PE partnerships. There are certain skills and mindsets that help entrepreneurs and corporate executives excel that do not naturally translate to a PE-backed portfolio company. A healthy ego means acknowledging a change in leadership—such as no longer being the top executive in your own business—if your business needs a different type of leadership for this new cycle. It means understanding that this does not affect the essence of who you really are.

GROWTH MINDSET

If you are an energetic founder or an executive with an entrepreneurial background, you may already have a growth business mindset. Regardless of where you are coming from, your PE venture will need you to tap into that growth mindset. If you are confident in yourself and your abilities and are willing and able to take up challenges that PE may present to you, this mindset will serve you well. That is because a thriving PE venture is not mundane or monotonous. You are in a state of continuous learning and are thrust into circumstances that require you to rise to the challenge. However, if your preference is more linear, and you find it far more comfortable when the business plateaus, this type of business may not be the most natural fit for you.

EMOTIONAL CONTROL

There is a certain level of emotional intelligence that's vital to the success of these partnerships with operators and the PE deal team that you will be working with. One of the key elements of emotional intelligence that you cannot do without is emotional control or emotional regulation. Emotionally controlled operators evaluate offers rationally and respond to setbacks professionally. They will pause, assess their emotions, and engage with processed responses. Now, we all know this to be the ideal approach, but as the famous philosopher Aristotle once stated, "Anyone can become angry—that is easy. But to be angry with the right person, to the right degree, at the right time, for the right purpose, and in the right way—that is not easy."[15]

---

15   Daniel Goleman, *Emotional Intelligence: Why It Can Matter More Than IQ* (Bantam Books, 1997).

If you notice your emotions have a bigger hold on you than you have on them, it is worth considering getting some form of assistance. Some operators turn to business coaches, others to therapists or psychologists. Regardless of what works for you, seek the assistance you need because out-of-control emotions can undo you and your team's hard work.

Let us consider the following illustration.

CASE STUDY
Kinko's, Inc., Founded by Paul Orfalea

Born in 1948, Paul Orfalea attended college at the University of California in the late 1960s. It was there that he was first inspired to start his business called Kinko's. This inspiration came to him on a visit to the college library, as he witnessed droves of students queuing to get copies of pages from books they wanted information from. A year before he completed his degree, he obtained a $5,000 bank loan. These preliminary funds allowed him to lease a garage located behind a taco stand, off the campus's main road. He also leased a Xerox photocopier, a printing press, and a film processing machine, with the goal of surveying which service would become the most profitable. He charged over 50 percent less than the university library for photocopying, and students flocked to his fledgling establishment. For added convenience for his customer base, he also sold stationery.[16]

---

16   "Orfalea, Paul," Encyclopedia.com, accessed November 3, 2025, https://www.encyclopedia.com/education/economics-magazines/orfalea-paul.

By 1979, Orfalea had grown his business to twenty-four storefronts. Four years later, he had eighty stores in a total of twenty-eight states. By the year 2000, the business was international, had 1,100 storefronts, and raked in $1 billion in revenue annually. At that point, his net worth was a quarter of a billion dollars. Over the lifespan of the enterprise, he received investments from different parties, with Orfalea eventually selling 30 percent interest in the company to an investment firm.[17]

If you have never heard of Orfalea until now, you might assume he had enjoyed smooth sailing to get himself to this point. On the contrary: In childhood, he experienced learning difficulties that were later diagnosed as dyslexia. The unique challenges that this presented led to him needing to adapt his approach to entrepreneurship. Without that adaptation, he likely would have failed.[18] In later interviews, Orfalea revealed that he also had ADHD, which added further complexity to his business journey.[19]

Yet, these challenges were not all Orfalea had to overcome. His background—coming from a business-orientated Lebanese family[20] and having advantages that his challenges forced him to cultivate—gave him an edge, especially when it came to sales and relationship manage-

---

17   Ibid.

18   Ibid.

19   Dan Schawbel, "Paul Orfalea on Creating the Kinko's Brand," *Forbes*, June 28, 2012, https://www.forbes.com/sites/danschawbel/2012/06/28/ paul-orfalea-on-creating-the-kinkos-brand/.

20   Ibid.

ment.[21] Yet, along the way, while working in his business, he discovered that he had significant anger issues to contend with. Largely due to the amount of intense pressure he was under because of cash flow concerns, he would sometimes find himself venting to his staff. On other occasions, he was inflamed by their conduct. In one example that Orfalea shared in his book, he literally ripped a sign off a store that he felt was antagonistic to customers. Fortunately, he realized that he needed to reign in his anger and dedicated time and effort toward harnessing his emotions.[22]

Eventually, Orfalea left the business to pursue other interests. However, do you think leaving his anger issues unresolved would have allowed him to enjoy the level of success that he did for more than thirty years?

JOINT LEADERSHIP

Once in the partnership, accepting that you will need to relinquish some level of control is crucial for mutual success.

As an entrepreneur, you likely had the last say. Now, you do not. As a division leader of a corporate enterprise, it was your profit and loss statement to manage. Now, it is not. That is your new (possibly uncomfortable) reality. The sooner you embrace that, the sooner you can start navigating this new territory that PE offers you.

---

21   Patrick O'Shaughnessy, host, *Invest Like the Best*, episode 299, "Paul Orfalea – It's About the Money," Spotify, October 18, 2022, https://open.spotify.com/episode/3x3xmrYHaFIUJsik4Ix0IJ.

22   Ibid., 00:49:00.

COLLABORATION IS KEY

With alignment of your values and vision, as well as joint leadership, you also need to orient yourself toward collaboration. It is one thing to agree on decision-making and management style. It is another to actively and positively participate in executing and implementing those decisions. In entrepreneurship, there is no context for collaboration or buy-in, because there are no operating partners and PE investors. After the sale, beyond making joint decisions and being on the same page, you must participate in the implementation of plans that you may not have wanted in the first place, regardless of their alignment with your values or vision. If you are transitioning from a corporate role, you are likely used to formal processes and bureaucracies established for decision-making. PE is a much faster paced environment in which the expectation is that decisions are made quickly, albeit thoughtfully and with the benefit of data.

Developing the Right Mindset

The practical application of the elements mentioned above means assessing your particular context and adjusting your shared strategies. Accepting the new and letting go of what no longer serves you and your business are part of your business's evolution to this next level. It means agreeing on cadence and maintaining it until you decide to improve it. It also involves accepting a period of developing rapport and working relationships with your new partners and partnership. The learning curve is steep initially but smoothens out with consistent effort.

PREREQUISITE KNOWLEDGE

Additionally, having some foundational knowledge before venturing into a PE relationship is helpful to achieve success. Operators must have a sound understanding of cash flow (compared to profitability), timelines, and debt financing as well as an analytical mindset. Though profits are naturally important, the PE firm pays significant attention to operating cash flow or earnings before interest, taxes, depreciation, and amortization (EBITDA). Prior to PE, operators typically do not consider a timeframe for wrapping up their involvement in a business. PE's typical five-year hold period creates urgency around every strategic decision.

Debt financing is normal at this level, or at any business level. Having some level of debt is a new reality that operators must get used to, as it is one of the ways that PE firms provide growth capital.

PE investors prioritize data-driven analysis over charisma or salesmanship. This approach is beneficial in the lifetime of your business and is worth cultivating because PE investors do not hold charisma and salesmanship in as high regard as the data and insights. Alignment of your perspectives can ease comprehension of the intentions and motives of PE partners as you navigate inevitable and uncomfortable changes.

Avoiding Common CEO Pitfalls

We looked at the mindset that is required for successful CEOs in PE businesses. PE investors who have been in the industry long enough end up having their own mindsets, priorities, goals, and timelines because of the perspective they possess. They can spot common founder behaviors and points of tactical friction that can derail the whole operation.

As we noted in the earlier case study, business as you know it is no longer the case. This creates all types of resistance. Following are some of the most common types of behaviors by operators who clash with PE firms.

EXCESSIVE SPENDING

Excessive spending signals that an operator hasn't accepted the new accountability structure. Luxury travel and unnecessary perks signal misaligned spending priorities. Often, those spending habits are not new. They are behavioral patterns exercised throughout the establishment and growth of the business prior to the sale. Excessive spending reflects the operator not yet having come to terms with the business no longer being just their own or with being accountable to someone else.

UNILATERAL DECISION-MAKING

In the past, some operators did not have to seek approval or consensus before hiring and firing. With a PE partnership, depending upon the level of the employee, such decisions may require authorization from the *deal team* members. Naturally, this world of oversight and decision-sharing is not always welcome. If a snap decision to hire or fire was the norm but now requires additional meetings, an extended operational hierarchy, and a potentially longer timeline, friction is no surprise.

CULTURAL CLASH

When the enterprise was in its growth phase, playing favorites and ambiguous reporting protocols and communication procedures may have been the norm. Maybe people felt unsafe to share their honest opinions and feedback for the benefit of the company, fearing backlash. All these are symptoms of a corporate culture that is incongruent with a business now owned by PE.

If you are the founder, you have significant influence on the culture of the business as you transition to PE. However, if you happen to be a CEO hired to lead going forward, you may find yourself faced with a culture that needs to adapt to succeed. When presented with such a situation, you must assess whether you and your team have the capacity to influence a shift in the company's culture. In some cases, you may decide that you may not be the best cultural fit or that you need help to make this new dynamic work.

Here is one example from my lived experience. Though not from a PE venture, it still illustrates the profound importance of a compatible culture fit.

CASE STUDY
Acceptable Decorum

Early in my career, I had just joined a profitable enterprise where I was excited to be of service. I was invited to attend a high-level meeting with executive management. I was still getting the lay of the land, so I reserved my contributions for important matters. As we sat gathered in the conference room, with the CEO presiding over the discourse, a relatively new employee decided to chime in. As it has been many years, I do not recall what question the CEO asked him to answer. Neither do I remember what the young gentleman said in response. I do, however, remember what happened next.

Suddenly, the CEO launched a pencil at this young man's head and managed to hit him with it.

Next, the CEO said, "That is probably the dumbest thing you've ever said, and I just met you, right?"

As if this was not surprising enough, the individual who had been hit in the head with the pencil apologized to the CEO.

"I'm sorry. I shouldn't have answered the question that way."

My shock did not end there, because I was instantly hit with two realizations. Firstly, people in this room thought this behavior was perfectly normal. Secondly, the person who had just been assaulted apologized for "causing" the assault.

Through this incident, I learned that I had found myself working in a toxic environment. And this was a culture I didn't want to be a part of. Regardless of how profitable this division was—with demonstrably great financial results—the way the team went about getting those results just wasn't for me.

Consequently, I quickly sought a new assignment outside of that division.

Perhaps we should ask ourselves, "Are there unhealthy behaviors that we need to root out to ensure the success of this PE transition?"

PE firms all have different cultures, just like entrepreneurial ventures have their own unique cultural persuasions. In the same vein, the partnerships your business forms with them will be unique because of these different approaches to working with portfolio companies and even managing their own firms. Let us look at another occasion when a misfit of culture presented itself. In this instance, it was at a PE venture.

CASE STUDY
Oh, That's Jack!

As you would, I applied to various opportunities throughout my PE career. Once, when I was midway in my career, I interviewed for a CEO role with a PE firm in New York. Naturally, the head of HR was responsible for administering my interview. I knew it was a challenging role, but I also knew I was up for the task. This interview was conducted in a small conference room that happened to be adjacent to another. Though the rooms were separated, neither was sufficiently soundproofed, a point that soon affected the outcome of my interview.

While my interview was underway, the head of HR made a call on the speakerphone. Over the phone, he informed another company executive that he had concluded our meeting and invited them to join us in the conference room to meet with me as well.

I then met with the second executive. As the head of HR had done before him, he called the switchboard and requested the next interviewee. As soon as that person hung up, a gentleman from the adjacent conference room torpedoed into our conference room.

"If you use that f**king speakerphone one more time, I'm going to rip that sh*t out of the wall," this stranger shouted, red-faced and breathing heavily. Almost as quick as he came, he returned to his conference room for his meeting.

The interviewer and I silently looked at this individual. I was shocked and puzzled. Once the irate man had left, the interviewer said, "Oh, that's Jack!" and brushed it aside.

It was made clear to me that this individual had a habit of flying off the handle and that it was so common that this was their normal. My problem was, I could not wrap my head around this being considered normal behavior in a professional setting.

At the conclusion of the process, I informed the head of the division that I didn't want to continue. I don't think that this culture was a viable fit. The disrespectful and mean-spirited nature of the brief incident that I witnessed was indicative of what would await me if I joined that PE firm. As for me, that was simply unacceptable behavior.

As an operator, it is vital you understand and fit into the culture. How do the management team and PE firm deal with adversity? Are they screaming and yelling? Or are they collaborative and constructive even amid disappointment?

CONTROL PREOCCUPATION

Control-obsessed CEOs block direct employee–investor communication. All high-level communication must be channeled through the founder or the new CEO. Any attempt at anything else will attract condemnation from the top executive. This behavior creates destructive organizational silos.

INADEQUATE PERFORMANCE

As an operator, you are committed to profitable growth. Consistently strong financial performance is key to success as an operator. Eventually, time proves when these commitments are not realized. With PE firms basing their decisions on these commitments, this leads the business to demonstrably low results.

PE Mindset

Then, there is the unique mindset that PE investors have. While passion and drive are admirable and are expected of good operators, the mindset of effective PE investors is vastly different. The most notable differences are priorities, timelines, and goals.

PRIORITIZING PROFESSIONALIZATION

Without a doubt, the main goal of PE is to effectively professionalize the business, especially for businesses that are small or first-time recipients of PE investment. PE investors aim to professionalize the business across the board, including finance, operations, customer relations, HR, branding and communication, legal and compliance, sales and marketing, measurement tools, and culture and leadership. In the age of technology, innovation is often the driver of these improvements. This frequently includes leveraging the benefits of technology and of other modern elements. Artificial intelligence (AI) is one such innovation that offers benefits to PE operations in multiple functions of the business.

Immediate infrastructure improvements earmarked during due diligence evaluation, before the sale, are top priorities. Is the company missing out because of outdated systems, such as manual processes that could be automated? Are there new revolutionary approaches to

HR? Is there a more efficient way to make payroll using automation? Could enterprise resource planning (ERP) software bring bountiful gains if rolled out? These types of changes for the purpose of making the organization more efficient are the focus of establishing a professional foundation.

Occasionally, engaging teams or independent consultants may be necessary to help achieve this goal.

But professionalism is not just about the tangible aspects of business; it's also about business relations.

TIMELINES

PE firms are acutely aware of the time constraints inherent in the PE business process. As stated in the introduction, the typical hold period is around five years. The planning that PE firms undergo with this understanding hinges on the development of a clear vision of the business's size, opportunities for diversification, and path to sustained profitability at exit.

Where an operator may default to seeing the timeline in a normal way—that is, forward progression—PE firms work backwards. They agree with the operator not only on the timeline but also on sales to profitability forecasts (formulating annual financial budgets). Most adjustments required are made annually. These adjustments could be due to outperforming expectations, macroeconomics, or competition. Plans are reassessed, and the performance matrix is analyzed on an annual basis, as well as monthly or quarterly, for an agreed-upon budget.

GOALS

The PE firm aims to maximize profits and improve margins where possible, just like the operator. It also aims to increase the *exit multiple*.

The exit multiple is *the price paid for a company as a function of a financial metric.*[23] Naturally, achieving monthly and annual financial goals is important for the eventual realization of longer-term goals and objectives.

What PE Firms Look for in Leadership

During the due diligence exercise, prior to striking a deal with the seller, the PE investors observe the leadership capabilities of the management team. If they assess that the team is strong and is likely to execute the growth plan, a fair amount of autonomy will be given. If the PE investors determine the team possesses poor leadership capabilities, but they still like the overall business and wish to proceed, they will incorporate mechanisms that mitigate this. Corrective measures may include engaging operating partners and beginning a search for replacements. The need for new management team members at the portfolio company is the reason why most corporate executives make the transition to PE.

Finally, among all the leadership skills that an operator possesses, adaptability may be key. PE firms know that as the business changes, what is needed from the operator might change too. As such, the business will need the operator to metaphorically shape-shift into what the business will become.

Best Practices for Partnership

No one likes bad news, but there's something worse: bad news that others find out that you should have shared with them. Your best call

---

23 "Entry Multiple," Corporate Finance Institute, accessed July 19, 2025, https://corporatefinanceinstitute.com/resources/valuation/entry-multiple/.

is to be as direct and as transparent as possible in your communication. If a loyal but underperforming long-term employee is contributing to significant unfavorable business outcomes, such as by careless handling of customer accounts or unnecessary expenditures, you need to let your PE partners know. Do not wait until you have addressed the problems that have been caused. You must inform your partners as soon as you realize how the employee's contribution to the business is impacting the company. Report all the metrics, not just the vital ones. You might, for example, find that the customer churn rate is creeping up while all other indicators remain positive. What if outside political or economic forces, such as increased tariffs, exacerbate the situation and cause even bigger problems? This is an issue PE partners want to see coming well in advance.

Also, avoiding erratic behavior will win you some support in the organization and from your partners. If you remain consistent in your demeanor, your PE partners know how to relate to you predictably. Predictability is an asset that most PE partners cherish. Grease the wheels of efficiency by being approachable, cultivating trustworthiness, and demonstrating a team spirit. Let your performance speak for itself over time, even through adversity.

CONCLUSION

In this chapter, we delved into the mindset of operators and PE investors. We examined the different mindsets and approaches to business growth that both possess. We also considered elements of a healthy mindset that operators need, how PE firms evaluate leadership capacity, and best practices for collaboration.

In the next chapter, we will look at something that many of us dread: rapid change, the transformation it brings about, and how you can manage it in your business.

KEY TAKEAWAYS

- Ensure you have shared values and a shared vision with the PE firm.
- Get grounded and sharpen your emotional and social intelligence by whatever means work best for you.
- Focus on collaboration, not on being the boss.
- Embrace professionalization.
- Curb unnecessary expenditure and be careful with your cash flow management.
- Foster open communication.
- Focus on your performance.

CHAPTER 2

ACCELERATING THROUGH TRANSFORMATION

High expectations are the key to everything.[24]

–SAM WALTON

Whether you're joining as an external executive or continuing as the founder, one thing is for sure: You now face enormous change. In the previous chapter, we assessed the mindset you need to achieve post-PE acquisition success. In this chapter, we will zero in on change or transformation management in your PE venture and the optimal pace for your efforts. We will discuss creating prioritization frameworks, PE financial literacy, evaluating your team's capabilities, changing strategies, relationship development, learning the business, and the PE timeline.

Before we delve into the subjects, here is a case study for us to draw preliminary insights from.

---

24 "100+ Entrepreneur Quotes," American Express, May 4, 2024, https:// www.americanexpress.com/en-us/business/blueprint/resource-center/ start/100-quotes-from-successful-entrepreneurs.

CASE STUDY
A Culture War

In one business experience of mine years ago, my predecessor expanded an enterprise into new markets. As the president of this company, he elected to sell the company's products to different and additional segments of the industry (business-to-consumer [B2C]).

Though the business was built on a different channel and market (business-to-business [B2B] model), it had a great market share and an outstanding brand. Throughout the company's history, it ran on B2B. My predecessor decided to extend toward a B2C model. Unfortunately, as there was inadequate buy-in from the sales team, many of the sales staff quit. Since the investment required to enter the B2C division was significant, the company ran into financial constraints, with the original B2B division suffering as a result. Not surprisingly, there was growing friction and a lack of harmony between B2B and B2C staff. After all, the financial diversion led each side to believe that their survival or success was somewhat threatened by the other, with the B2B staff feeling underinvested in and ignored. We could even say a culture war ensued.

When I took the helm, I assessed the situation and evaluated the strategy. It was clear to me that the enterprise had to shift back to its core business. This meant writing off several investments and letting go of some team members. So, not only did I need the business to stop hemorrhaging money, but I also had to take it back to its core competencies.

When I reflect on this experience, I realize that it was a time of intense change management and decisive action. Letting go of an endeavor that people once believed in but is failing may be challenging, but that's the decision leadership must make. Laying off loyal employees when the company can no longer afford them is also part of the job. In times of change, these are some of the decisions that need to be made quickly.

In addition, this experience highlighted to me that it is unwise to presume that the strategy a predecessor employed should be maintained. You must ask yourself, "Is this strategy ideal for attaining the results the business needs? If not, what is a better way for optimal success?"

Lastly, it's worth asking yourself, "Am I making transformative decisions at a pace that is conducive to the business surviving and, ultimately, thriving?"

With this Culture War case study touching upon some of the key topics we will discuss, let us begin by briefly assessing the necessity of creating prioritization frameworks for your PE venture.

Creating Prioritization Frameworks

In planning the sale, leadership (the operator and PE partners) agrees on what the most pertinent initiatives will be within a given period after the sale. Often, the timeline for implementation of primary priorities is the first 90 or 120 days. Identifying your top work streams (distinct areas of focus) and processes is one of the primary decisions the operators and PE partners need to make. This could be the integration of new systems and processes. If PE investment is anticipated for new systems such as ERP, payroll, customer relationship management (CRM), HR, etc., it is necessary to plan and implement efficiently. It could be a go-to-market or sales-related initiative. It could also be a more operational plan to improve or rectify a fault, such as inventory management or logistics concerns.

As is often the case in busy growing enterprises, even as you prioritize, you may have too many goals legitimately vying for importance and prioritization. Therefore, it is imperative that you develop the skills of turning down opportunities, pushing back, and accepting your team's limitations when there are too many priorities to execute well. In these cases, you need to focus on two or three priorities, address them successfully, and then move on to the next set of top priorities.

Operators must have a clear understanding of what these top priorities are, and the execution required for the same. Certain initiatives demand immediate attention and careful prioritization. Typically, there are few priorities for most businesses. As each business is different, you will have to determine these priorities for yourself.

PE Financial Literacy

Creating an effective prioritization framework is necessary to manage your business's transformation, but financial literacy may be even more important. At the same time, financial literacy is one thing, and PE financial literacy is another. No one expects the operator to have the training or financial savvy of a seasoned PE investor. Rather, the expectation is that operators know what the key metrics are (moving forward) and understand what they mean, how they are calculated, and how to impact them.

Early on, you must understand and discuss with the PE partners the metrics, the drivers of these metrics, and the expectations related to these metrics to maximize your business's overall performance. Some of the metrics may include revenue, gross margins, and EBITDA.

You must know the drivers of EBITDA, how working capital is consumed, the activities that impact these metrics, and what you can do to achieve the best outcomes. These are just a few examples of performance metrics that you will need to agree on with your PE partners and other relevant stakeholders.

Evaluation of the Capabilities of the Team

Regardless of the strategy you choose to employ, you need to make a timely determination that you have the right team for the task at hand. With careful analysis, you might realize that the answer is different from what you first assumed. We will address the capabilities of the team in chapter 4, "Your Team May Need an Upgrade."

Just as the operator evaluates the capabilities of the team, the PE partners do the same. Typically, this evaluation may be ongoing for up to one year post-sale. One year may sound longer than necessary, but the reality is that a shorter period would not unearth all the realities of the business. Much like in a marriage in which the couple enjoys the honeymoon period initially, but there comes a time when the fullness of the realities of married life starts to become apparent.

The post-sale PE business experience is similar in that the various parties have met and had all the necessary conversations, the PE partners have toured the business premises, and they may even have had several business dinners together. However, how the business truly operates daily remains somewhat unknown. For that reason, the capabilities of the team continue to be evaluated, with factors assessed from the PE perspective being like those assessed from the operator perspective that we have already discussed. Surprises might arise, or known considerations that were not genuinely understood might unearth a different reality and cause alarm or demand attention. Regardless of what the issue is, you can often only learn it over time—once the honeymoon period is over. Until then, the PE partner typically gives the operators the benefit of the doubt.

Re-Strategizing

As management, you need to assess the way the business strategy was executed and determine if it is sensible and sufficient for current expectations. If your assessment shows you that your approach is too slow or deficient, work more efficiently or change your approach entirely. Perhaps your assessment reveals that your strategy still works, but incoming data suggests detrimental trends, and you must decide on whether your existing efforts need to change considering new insights.

Regardless of what strategy you utilize, you will need to determine if the business has all the capabilities in key functional areas that it needs to drive the strategy. It is wise to approach these assessments with open-mindedness because it is not uncommon for an operator to assume the business has all the key staff and partners for the selected strategy, only to eventually come across a surprising (and sometimes expensive) hurdle that proves otherwise.

Therefore, operators would be wise to ask themselves a few probing questions, such as "Are we going to conduct our activities in the same way for the investment capital that's coming into the business? If we are trying to grow faster, aiming for increased profitability, or trying to gain more market share, will this be achieved by conducting business as we have always done?"

If you reflect on these questions and your answers are "Yes," it then begs the question, "If you could have all along, why didn't you?" From my experience, the honest answer is to opt for new paths and new decisions. Typically, there must be some sort of change that enables you to achieve the next level of business success. Strategizing may mean allocating more or better resources to improve outcomes. This may mean augmenting the capabilities of your team or even increasing your business's capital. It is worth noting that increasing the capabilities of your team does not necessarily mean more people; it just means more of the right skills or capabilities must be available in your team.

To illustrate this point further, consider the following case study.

CASE STUDY
Horizon Bradco and PE

In 1987, Horizon Bradco, a New York–based HVAC service provider and commercial food equipment business, was born.[25] Formed organically by several family-owned businesses, the company grew through acquisitions.[26] Continuous expansion led to the company becoming a regional contender with four locations and a labor force of over three hundred people. It benefited from its slow yet adaptive pace and decentralized system, which allowed

---

25   "Horizon Bradco Overview," PitchBook, accessed August 17, 2025, https://pitchbook.com/profiles/company/58377-52#overview.

26   Mark Kesti, "[Case Study] How a Private Equity Portfolio Company Created a Turnaround Success," Innovosales, February 15, 2022, https://innovosales.com/blog/case-study-how-a-private-equity-portfolio-company-created-a-turnaround-success/.

each acquired business its own sales team, processes, and relationship-centric decision-making focused on local markets.

When Horizon Bradco received PE investment, this investment was significant, so much so that the old way of doing business, particularly the decentralized approach, was no longer effective. Rapid quarter-over-quarter sales growth was needed to boost EBITDA and eventually ensure a successful exit by the end of the holding period.[27] The success of the PE approach depended on standardized systems and loan repayment periods, but this was unattainable since acquired companies retained their sales team and processes, leading to a lack of sales metrics.[28] What's more, the sales teams were not being trained, particularly in cross-selling or product upselling.[29]

The PE firm wanted immediate results. Revenues were unsatisfactory. In fact, even before the COVID-19 pandemic, the bank wanted its money back.[30]

Was failure imminent?

The situation demanded immediate action, which the VP of sales delivered effectively.[31] The once decentralized sales teams were unified. A CRM tool was deployed. Members of the sales team were given weekly coaching,

---

27   Iris Dorbian, "Audax-Backed Smart Care Buys Horizon Bradco," PE Hub, August 30, 2021, https://www.pehub.com/audax-backed-smart-care-buys-horizon-bradco/.

28   Kesti, "[Case Study] Private Equity Portfolio."

29   Ibid.

30   Ibid.

31   Ibid.

and a collaborative compensation plan was agreed on and implemented. All these efforts and more led to a boost of 16 percent in sales year over year and ultimately led to a successful acquisition by Smart Care Equipment, backed by Audax.[32]

Consider Horizon Bradco's approach. Would the company have survived and thrived if the management team had not strategized and opted to make changes that included standardizing and moving away from a decentralized approach?

Relationship Development

As you will see in this chapter, almost all the mentioned aspects must be implemented relatively quickly. Relationship development is no different. Though building relationships is a long-term endeavor, your efforts at establishing and maintaining effective business relationships are paramount. Relationship building requires careful and deliberate work. Trust, a key ingredient in healthy relationships—including those in the business arena—depends on your concerted and sustained efforts. You will have to develop a cadence with your partners. You may need to make some accommodations for your business relationship to work. It is also likely that you will have to exercise flexibility. This might involve being more gracious with PE partners who expect you to be available for sporadic business calls outside planned virtual meetings. It might mean scheduling online meetings at a time that's more amenable to them, if you happen to be across the world from them. These accommodations and the proposed flexibility might be new to you, and they might not be

---

32   Ibid.

ideal. However, the approach will no doubt go a long way in nurturing goodwill and strengthening relations.

As with any new relationship, you may have the occasional awkward moment. That is to be expected with any two people or parties who have only just come to know each other. To build this relationship, it will benefit you to assert who your new partners are as individuals. Identify what their styles and idiosyncrasies are. Do they prefer taking your calls in the morning or in the afternoon? Do they prefer emails to phone calls? Are there specific conversations that they prefer to have face-to-face before anything else? If you are a busy operator and tend to prefer texting while you are on the go, but your PE partners prefer emails, you will have to decide who will make accommodations for the sake of the health of this working relationship.

Consider the following case study.

CASE STUDY
Joe & The Juice

Joe & The Juice is a juice bar that was founded in Denmark by Kaspar Basse, a former karate champion, in 2002. From its inception, its patrons enjoyed the business's customer-centric approach, fruit drinks, and trendy yet casual branding and style. The company championed staff contributions and invested in the success of the culture of the business and its innovations.[33]

In 2013, Joe & The Juice obtained private investment from Valedo Partners, a Swedish PE firm, with the goal of

---

33   "Joe History," Joe & The Juice, accessed August 18, 2025, https://www.joejuice.com/culture/joe-history.

global expansion.[34] Over the next ten years, the company expanded to become a global contender, growing from 50 stores to 350 during this period.[35] Its manpower grew from hundreds of employees to thousands. More impressively, its revenue rose from $23.51 million domestically to $360.41 million (conversion rate of 1 DKK = $0.1567[36]) in all markets by the end of that decade.[37]

However, this decade of rapid growth was not without its hurdles. Among the challenges during this expansion phase were employee retention[38] and maintaining the company's unique culture.[39] In recognition of the complexities of global expansion and sustaining the company culture, management prioritized maintaining that culture:

> *According to Kaspar Basse, the challenge is to channel the spirit of the company into a rapidly expanding workforce. To counteract a potential shift in culture, Joe & The Juice have established the SWAT-team. By assembling a group of top performing employees, willing to travel the world, the company is able to provide control and a high level*

34   "General Atlantic Agrees to Buy Majority Stake in Joe & The Juice," *Bloomberg*, November 13, 2023, https://www.bloomberg.com/news/articles/2023-11-13/ general-atlantic-agrees-to-buy-majority-stake-in-joe-the-juice.

35   "Joe & The Juice," Valedo Partners, accessed August 18, 2025, https://www. valedopartners.com/en/joe-the-juice/.

36   "DKK to USD," Exchange-Rates.org, last modified August 18, 2025, https://www. exchange-rates.org.

37   Valedo Partners, "Joe & The Juice."

38   Ethan Rouen and Suraj Srinivasan, "Joe & The Juice Crosses the Atlantic," Harvard Business School Multimedia/Video Case 118-039, November 2017, https://www.hbs. edu/faculty/Pages/item.aspx?num=53585.

39   "A Curious Case in Culture – Kaspar Basse, Founder of Joe & The Juice," Les Deux, accessed August 18, 2025, https://lesdeux.com/blogs/explore/ kaspar-basse-founder-of-joe-and-the-juice-a-curious-case-in-culture.

> *of care for their new locations. They reach out to new markets and ensure that the Joe & The Juice approach is transferred properly, and that the culture lives on.*[40]

With innovative administrative systems, the company managed to create a framework that helped attract employees who likely best aligned with the company's ethos and culture:

> *Basse says staffers feel a particular sense of ownership since they know they have a future with the company. At Joe & The Juice, 99% of mid- and top management started out as juicers. The upward mobility has transformed the way the company hires and how staff regard their jobs.*
>
> *So, how does one become part of the Joe & The Juice team? Via a rigorous, structured recruitment program known as "casting." "It's very functional, fun exercises over the course of a few hours," Basse says.*
>
> *Potential hires partake in various social, personal, and physical tests ranging from how fast they can operate a juicer to how well they can chitchat.*[41]

You may note that Joe & The Juice managed to accomplish something unique despite global expansion. They managed to maintain a company culture and spirit very similar to that of the entrepreneurship venture that the business started off as.

---

40 Ibid.

41 Rina Raphael, "Coffee, Sandwich, and a Side of Edgy: How Joe & The Juice Aims to Take Over the U.S.," *Fast Company*, January 11, 2017, https://www.fastcompany.com/3066489/coffee-sandwich-and-a-side-of-edgy-how-joe-the-juice-aims-to-take-over-the.

The dynamics associated with the operator perspective of relationship development are like those of the PE perspective, with a few differences. The reality is that operators often must acquiesce in this dynamic business relationship. One of the reasons this is the case is that, typically, the PE deal team may have several other portfolio companies that they manage. As such, they typically attempt to standardize practices by conducting business very similar across the board. Their goal throughout their portfolio is to make and keep their responsibilities manageable.

Therefore, the PE partner is likely going to dictate communication protocols to some extent. However, PE partners are also in a unique position to learn more about the management team's levels of emotional and social intelligence. The PE partner is tasked with ensuring that management conducts themselves in a manner that is constructive for mutual success, such as offering constructive criticism to the CEO, when necessary, with the goal of improving the business. This is a skill that requires awareness of one's impact on the other party: Overly critical feedback may destroy the confidence of the management team, yet feedback on the other extreme may be so ineffective that the team fails to improve their performance. Therefore, since everyone is a unique individual with different personalities and management styles, the PE partner must develop the emotional and social stamina to effectively navigate these dynamics and must develop the right communication style for prime effectiveness. Again, this is yet another aspect to fully realize early on.

Learn the Business

PE partners or guides are not operators. That is why operators and other experts are vital to the success of the PE venture. Operators are the people who understand the intricacies of the business. In comparison, PE partners may understand the business at a more theoretical level. After all the site visits, PowerPoint presentations, and management meetings, the PE partner is now working with parties who may have decades of experience in the business. As encouraging as that may be, it is still necessary for PE partners to assess the operator's efforts with a level of discernment. As the famous proverb goes, "Trust, but verify."[42]

Often, PE partners are relatively young and may be underestimated by operators who are more advanced in age and operational experience. What is important for operators to keep in mind is while their age and the operational experience that they possess are indeed important, so is what the PE professional brings to the table. When these factors are glaringly apparent, this is a complex dynamic that requires significant emotional intelligence to manage and successfully navigate.

The PE Timelines

In my experience, the PE timeline typically spans approximately five years and can be segmented into three distinct phases. These three phases are the fix phase, the growth phase, and the expand phase.

THE FIX PHASE

This phase often spans from the first to the second year. Your goal during this period is to fix the business by professionalizing and upgrading infrastructure at all levels: talent, processes, and people levels. If your intention is, for example, regional or global expansion or simply share leadership in your local or national market, you must

---

42   Gardiner Morse, "Trust, but Verify," *Harvard Business Review*, May 2005, https://hbr. org/2005/05/trust-but-verify.

provide a sturdier foundation for the operation to thrive on. Therefore, that may mean upgrading the management team or implementing any enhancements to the operation through professionalization or improved infrastructure.

Milestones for this phase often include reaching operational stability, realizing cost savings, and restoring positive cash flow. To achieve any of these milestones, conducting due diligence and audits is of primary importance. This is typically followed by restructuring the company's hierarchy and eliminating redundancies. The optimization of the supply chain and of working capital is another integral step toward a successful fix phase.

THE GROWTH PHASE

Now that the proper infrastructure is in place, you can focus on growth. This phase typically lasts from the third to fourth year but may be longer or shorter depending on your business's unique set of circumstances. In addition, it may overlap with another phase. Your attention, as management, is on how to grow the business organically, how to close more deals, and how to achieve greater market share. You can now leverage your new talent, tools, and processes to accelerate the profitable growth of the business.

Hitting revenue growth targets, achieving desired market share expansion, and realizing improvements in profit margins are among the milestones your company may reach during this phase. Key to realizing these milestones is investing in sales, marketing, and research and development. Enhancing your catalog of products or services and attending to your customer acquisition and retention initiatives are equally essential business activities in this phase.

THE EXPAND PHASE

The final phase is the expand phase. In this phase, investment is directed toward new markets, new trades, and other aspects of the business that make it different.

Once you are near or at this phase, you will have started to think about your exit. This is the prime time because you are at a point where you can demonstrably present how you have fixed the business, professionalized it, implemented infrastructural upgrades, and subsequently reaped the benefits. At this point, the benefits should include increased market share and profitability, so it makes financial sense for potential buyers to consider acquiring.

In this phase, milestones include completed and successful mergers and acquisitions (M&A) integrations; profitable diversification of the company's goods or services; and the formation of a high-performing, cohesive management team that has the capacity for continued growth.

I would be remiss to conclude this chapter without discussing the following beloved brand.

CASE STUDY
Toys"R"Us

You may have heard of Toys"R"Us but maybe not of its founder, Charles Lazarus. Lazarus's father owned a bike shop in Washington, DC, and in 1948, he began selling baby furniture in his father's shop and later included toys in the stock. Presumably, because of successful sales, the shop was renamed Children's Supermart. A few years later, Lazarus opened his first baby furniture and toy supermarket. In 1957, he named the store Toys"R"Us. In 1966, he sold his four stores to Interstate Stores, Inc. but continued to manage the enterprise. By 1974, the chain had grown to a total of fifty-one branches, but the parent company—Interstate—suddenly went bankrupt. Four years later, the company restructured, selling off much of its other business interests but managing to retain sixty-three toy stores. At this point, it was decided to rename the company Toys"R"Us, Inc.[43]

At its peak, which was in the '90s, Toys"R"Us had over 1,400 stores. However, the company had to file for bankruptcy in 2017, leading to the closure of all the business's US stores.[44]

At this point in the downward trajectory, the business was "earning" a return on equity of negative 47.37 percent for its shareholders. Critics have posited that this may have been caused by its shrinking market share as a result of the arrival and growth of Amazon and other smaller boutique toy stores or by the debt the company raked up while it was a PE venture with Bain Capital.[45]

One Harvard-based commentator stated the following about the demise of Toys"R"Us:

---

43   "Toys 'R' Us, Inc. History," Funding Universe, accessed November 5, 2025, https://www.fundinguniverse.com/company-histories/toys-r-us-inc-history/.

44   Tom Ryan, "Should Toys'R'Us Be Toying with Flagships Again?" RetailWire, October 5, 2023, https://retailwire.com/discussion/should-toysrus-be-toying-with-flagships-again/.

45   Brian Misamore, "Breaking Down the Demise of Toys 'R' Us," *Harvard Business School Online*, April 10, 2018, https://online.hbs.edu/blog/post/breaking-down-the-demise-of-toys-r-us.

Let's look again at Toys "R" Us. They have two big glaring problems – one, their Net Margin is negative, they are losing money. This is the effect of competition and the toy-market squeeze mentioned earlier. Second, they have an incredibly high debt load – an equity multiplier of 5.35. This is a consequence of Bain Capital's purchase and sale of them in the early 2000s – private equity often adds a high amount of debt to companies in order to generate returns for its investors. Often, the companies are selected based on their reliable, stable returns – in other words, they can often pay this debt load without trouble, and Toys "R" Us in 2005 likely seemed to be such a company.

This analysis suggests that the debt alone wasn't enough to destroy the company. The debt just multiplies whatever is happening with the other two values. That meant, when things went wrong, they went really wrong. A combination of both competitive pressure and high debt load was required to bring about the end of Toys "R" Us.[46]

With my experience in PE, I imagine that the debt the company accrued during its time under PE ownership was perpetuated by quick changes to expedite profitability. Paying off the interest on the money the business loaned must have lagged growth, and with the extra fees that are often paid to the owners, the company struggled to keep up as it hemorrhaged financially.

The pace of change and the financial demands were simply incompatible.

---

46   Ibid.

CONCLUSION

In this chapter, we explored some of the complexities of change management in a PE venture. We also briefly touched upon PE financial literacy and the importance for operators of mastering this skill. In the next chapter, we will take a closer look at the financial metrics that are integral to your business's success.

KEY TAKEAWAYS

- The pace of change in PE ventures is different from that in entrepreneurship, and you must adjust accordingly.
- PE ventures have many aspects that need your diligent attention. You must organize your efforts and execute expeditiously.
- Relationships are an ongoing and continuous investment. You must do what it takes to earn and maintain trust.
- Do not be afraid of changing a strategy that no longer serves the interest of the current investment and management teams.

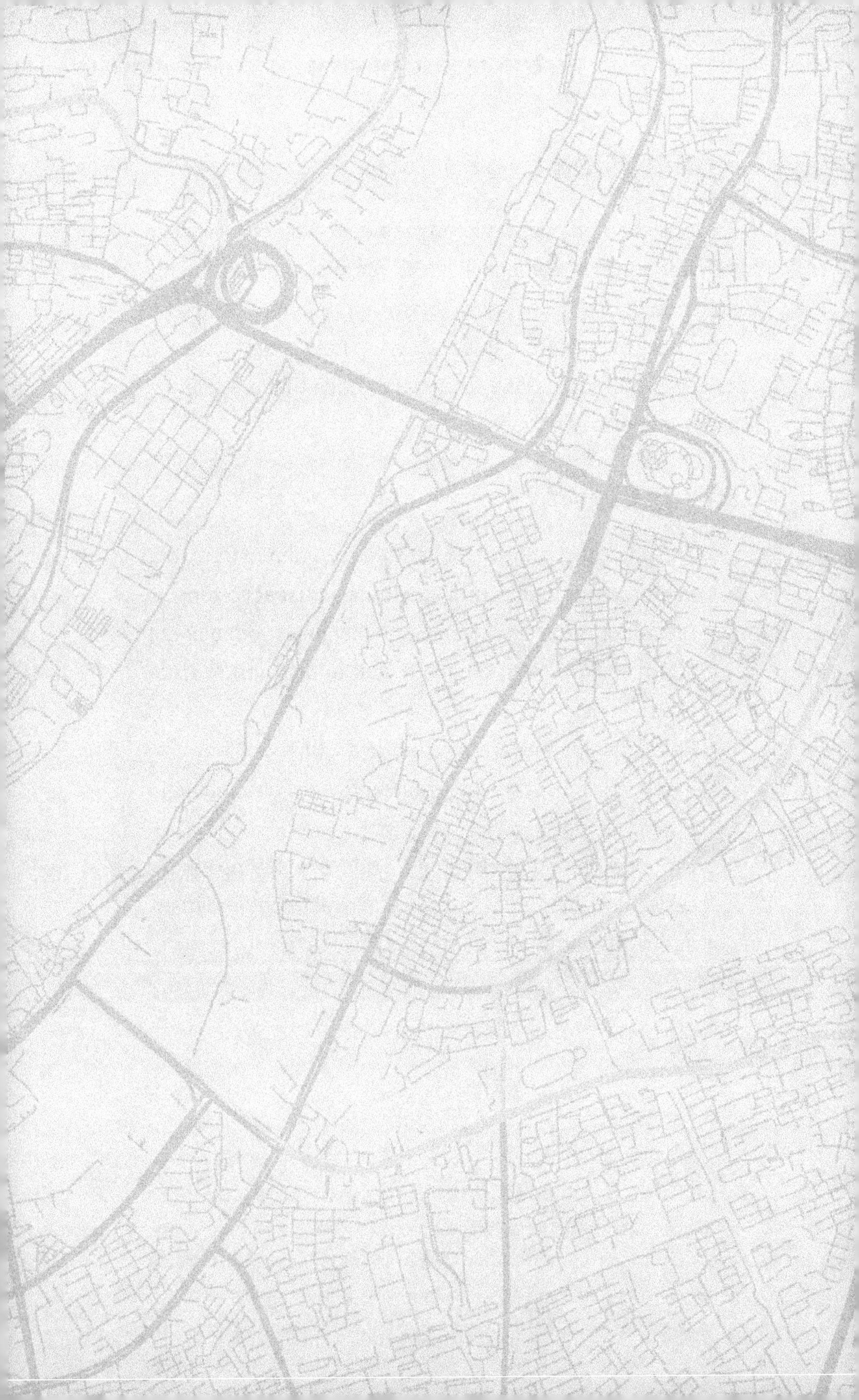

CHAPTER 3

MASTERING PE FINANCIAL LANGUAGE

An investment in knowledge pays the best interest.[47]

–BENJAMIN FRANKLIN

In chapter 1, we discussed the mindsets that are ideal for the business success of the management team and the PE partners. In chapter 2, we looked at how to effectively manage change in your PE business throughout its different phases. In this chapter, we focus on the financial metrics or key performance indicators (KPIs) that are important in this type of business. Some of these may even be new to you. I encourage you to learn and understand the terms in this chapter. In the same vein, mastering PE financial language is as important for your venture as having a high-quality CFO at the reins of the business's financial PE journey.

---

47   David Bakke, "The Top 25 Investing Quotes of All Time," Investopedia, last updated September 3, 2025, https://www.investopedia.com/financial-edge/0511/the-top-17-investing-quotes-of-all-time.aspx.

Before we take a closer look at the individual perspectives of the operator and the PE partner, it is important to understand how alignment on performance will be measured, how investments will be made, and how that's probably different from how a seller or corporate investor may have approached this before.

Key Performance Indicators

KPIs measure "a company's overall long-term performance against a set of targets, objectives, or industry peers."[48] If you were an entrepreneur, you likely focused on revenue growth,[49] customer acquisition cost (CAC),[50] customer lifetime value (CLV),[51] burn rate,[52] customer retention rate (CRR),[53] net promoter scale (NPS),[54] monthly active

---

48   "KPIs: What Are Key Performance Indicators? Types and Examples," Investopedia, last updated June 17, 2025, https://www.investopedia.com/terms/k/kpi.asp.

49   Steve Blank, "The Four Steps to the Epiphany: Measuring Progress in Startups," *Harvard Business Review*, February 2013, https://hbr.org/2013/02/the-four-steps-to-the-epiphany.

50   Brad Feld, "Why Customer Acquisition Cost Is the Most Important Metric for Startups," *Forbes*, August 15, 2019, https://www.forbes.com/sites/forbesfinancecouncil/2019/08/15/why-customer-acquisition-cost-is-the-most-important-metric-for-startups/.

51   "Growing Faster Than Your Competitors: The Role of Customer Lifetime Value," McKinsey & Company, accessed August 24, 2025, https://www.mckinsey.com/business-functions/marketing-and-sales/our-insights/growing-faster-than-your-competitors.

52   Neil Patel, "Understanding Burn Rate: A Critical Metric for Startups," *Entrepreneur*, June 10, 2020, https://www.entrepreneur.com/article/351684.

53   "Customer Retention: The Key to Startup Success," Bain & Company, accessed August 24, 2025, https://www.bain.com/insights/customer-retention-the-key-to-startup-success/.

54   Frederick Reichheld, "The One Number You Need to Grow," *Harvard Business Review*, December 2003, https://hbr.org/2003/12/the-one-number-you-need-to-grow.

users (MAU), daily active users (DAU),[55] gross margin,[56] and other such KPIs. As the business is now a PE venture, some of the most vital KPIs will be different from those you have utilized before, and others may be entirely new to you. However, it is imperative that you understand that the KPIs that are relevant will vary from industry to industry and from business to business. The KPIs that you measure and monitor depend entirely on your unique situation.

Regardless, we will take a moment to look at some of the most common KPIs that you may encounter and may find vital in your venture. This list is by no means exhaustive or concrete. This is a general exercise to help familiarize you with what you may come across, which can include the following: internal rate of return (IRR),[57] multiple on invested capital (MOIC),[58] cash flow metrics,[59] EBITDA,[60] revenue

---

55   Kim-Mai Cutler, "Why Active Users Are the Lifeblood of Startups," TechCrunch, March 12, 2018, https://techcrunch.com/2018/03/12/why-active-users-are-the-lifeblood-of-startups/.

56   "Startup Success: Key Financial Metrics for Entrepreneurs," Deloitte, accessed August 24, 2025, https://www.deloitte.com/us/en/insights/industry/technology/startup-financial-metrics.html.

57   Jason Fernando, "Internal Rate of Return (IRR): Formula and Examples," Investopedia, accessed August 24, 2025, https://www.investopedia.com/terms/i/irr.asp.

58   "MOIC and IRR: Key Metrics in Private Equity," PitchBook, accessed August 24, 2025, https://pitchbook.com/news/articles/moic-and-irr-key-metrics-in-private-equity.

59   "Private Equity Value Creation: The Power of Operational Excellence," Bain & Company, accessed August 24, 2025, https://www.bain.com/insights/private-equity-value-creation-global-private-equity-report-2023/.

60   "Value Creation in Private Equity," McKinsey & Company, accessed August 24, 2025, https://www.mckinsey.com/business-functions/strategy-and-corporate-finance/our-insights/value-creation-in-private-equity.

growth,[61] leverage ratios,[62] portfolio company operational metrics,[63] and exit multiples.[64] It is worth noting that, next, I utilize several examples to illustrate my points, examples that are all hypothetical. Many of these terms and concepts are far more complex. However, I have opted to simplify them to create an easy introduction in case these terms are new to you. I encourage you to seek more advanced sources for a more in-depth understanding of these terminologies.

IRR is the indicator that you use to assess the annual rate of return from the business's investment in relation to the time value of money.[65] If your business received $2 million in PE investment, and the venture attained a 19 percent IRR, that means your venture grew by 19 percent.

- *MOIC* is an indicator that quantifies the returns generated from an investment in proportion to the amount of capital initially invested.[66] If the PE firm invests $2 million and subsequently generates $10 million in return, then the MOIC is 5×.
- *Cash flow metrics* include free cash flow (FCF) and operating cash flow. *FCF* assesses the cash you retain after you deduct

---

61   "Private Equity: Driving Value Creation in Portfolio Companies," Deloitte, accessed August 24, 2025, https://www.deloitte.com/us/en/insights/industry/financial-services/private-equity-value-creation.html.

62   "Leverage Metrics in Private Equity: A Focus on Debt-to-EBITDA," S&P Global, accessed August 24, 2025, https://www.spglobal.com/marketintelligence/en/news-insights/research/leverage-metrics-in-private-equity.

63   "Private Equity: Unlocking Value Through Operational Excellence," PwC, accessed August 24, 2025, https://www.pwc.com/gx/en/services/advisory/deals/private-equity/value-creation.html.

64   *Global Private Equity Exit Report 2023* (EY, 2023), https://www.ey.com/en_gl/private-equity/exit-strategy.

65   Fernando, "Internal Rate of Return (IRR)."

66   "Maximizing Returns: Understanding MOIC in Private Equity," CFI, accessed November 10, 2025, https://corporatefinanceinstitute.com/resources/wealth-management/moic-private-equity/.

capital expenditure, while *operating cash flow* measures cash from the core business operations.[67]

- *EBITDA* is an indicator that excludes nonoperating expenses (interest, taxes, depreciation, and amortization) in its calculation of a portfolio company's profitability.[68]

- *Revenue growth*, measured as a percentage over a given period, is an indicator of a PE venture's top-line revenue.[69] Revenue is sometimes referred to as Sales or Turnover.

- *Leverage ratios* include *debt-to-EBITDA*, which is a metric arrived at by measuring the difference between the total debt and EBITDA of the venture.[70] For example, if your company has $5 million in debt and $1 million in EBITDA, then the venture has a debt-to-EBITDA ratio of 5×.

- *Portfolio company operational metrics* are business performance data at the operational level and include KPIs such as CAC, churn rate, production efficiency, and CLV.[71] In a Silicon Valley tech venture, CAC (how much it costs to acquire a new paying user or customer) is crucial to monitor.

- *Exit multiples,* such as enterprise value (EV)/EBITDA or EV/revenue, are presented as multiples of the portfolio company's revenues or earnings and measure the business's sale value. They indicate how much it costs the buyer, in relation to the business's financial performance.[72]

---

67   Bain & Company, "Private Equity Value Creation."

68   McKinsey & Company, "Value Creation in Private Equity."

69   Deloitte, "Private Equity: Driving Value Creation."

70   S&P Global, "Leverage Metrics in Private Equity."

71   PwC, "Private Equity: Unlocking Value."

72   EY, *Global Private Equity Exit Report 2023*.

In addition, there may be KPIs to monitor growth rates or improvement rates in comparison with previous periods. These may include revenue, gross margins, and operating expenses from prior periods, adjusted EBITDA, and metrics related to working capital dynamics. Going forward, all these metrics are still important, but there is additional focus on other metrics such as those expounded upon in this section, especially those related to operating expenses and operating cash flow. Adjusted EBITDA, though, is the ultimate profitability gauge of a portfolio company.

Adjusting to the New Metrics

As already highlighted, the metrics that will be important to the PE venture may be very different from the ones that have been outlined. Each venture is different, and it is important to be cognizant of that. Regardless of which metrics are important to your venture and to your PE partners, there is a process your PE partners will use to measure metrics. PE ventures typically measure different metrics than the ones business leaders were using while the firm was an entrepreneurship business.

In entrepreneurship, there is heavy reliance on sales metrics to assess performance. The leadership team may also pay concerted attention to gross margin.

Observations of business operations highlight that most operators enter the PE venture with a sales, commercial, or technical orientation. They are often exceptional at managing customer relations, with charisma and excellent communication skills. At the same time, they lack the financial sophistication that they need to wield when their business makes the transition to the PE phase. In such cases, beyond operators undergoing PE financial literacy training, it may be necessary to employ additional personnel to fill that gap.

The operator should do whatever they must to become conversant with all the new financial metrics relevant to their venture (i.e., attain PE financial literacy). This may mean asking the PE firm for assistance in better understanding the key matrices and how they are calculated. Most firms will be happy to spend time with the management team to fill any knowledge gaps.

Alternatively, you may wish to consider other means of acquiring knowledge about these new metrics. Courses, mentorship, the PE partners, and even artificial technology and other innovations are all possible alternatives. There are numerous courses; many are available online or even at universities, offering boot camps or similar types of training for several weeks. There, operators can learn with peers in a class environment. Mentorship from someone experienced in a similar leadership role or an individual willing to assist you in a buddy system arrangement can assist in your growth process as you become conversant with the array of new financial metrics. The individuals that either mentor, coach, or provide general support would be professionals with functional expertise in your type of business. Individuals in the PE firm who have firsthand experience with your type of business may also be a wealth of knowledge. They might welcome the opportunity to familiarize the management team with relevant metrics and how they are calculated.

If all those alternatives are unsuitable, consider utilizing technology; for example, online knowledge-sharing services such as YouTube or even AI. There are endless AI services you could try, including ChatGPT, Grok, Claude.AI, and DeepSeek. Regardless of which service you use, make sure to confirm the credibility of the information that it generates, as AI has been known to occasionally present inaccurate information and AI hallucinations, a type of incorrect information fabricated by AI and initially presented as factual.[73] Ultimately, whatever approach is best for you is the approach that is uniquely suited to how you best acquire knowledge.

It is incumbent on the management team to keep in mind that PE firms almost always use debt financing. As such, the PE venture must have cash flow available (i.e., operating cash flow to pay all the company's bills and to service the interest expense on the debt). Most operators who are coming into PE ventures for the first time have not had to manage their profit and loss statement and balance sheet in this manner. In some cases, these operators used to pay themselves dividends whenever they chose to. This type of unilateral decision is no longer an option. As a PE venture, founders may need to wait until the end of the year, after the financial statements are audited for incentive compensation. The board will then assess senior leadership's performance against the budget and determine if bonuses are deserved or not. Largely, variable compensation will be predicated on delivering against the company's budget and actual performance.

PE partners expect the operators to understand how PE firms look at different profit and loss statements and balance sheet numbers. They want the management team to fully grasp how they assess the performance of the business so that they can have fruitful, meaningful, and intelligent dialogue. In any conversation, let alone contractual obligation, if one person doesn't understand what the other person is asking or expecting, it is hard to have a meaningful discussion. To that end, most PE firms would be happy to task someone knowledgeable within the team to help the operator become conversant in this area.

---

73 "What Are AI Hallucinations?" IBM, accessed August 24, 2025, https://www.ibm. com/think/topics/ai-hallucinations.

The PE firm does not expect the operators to understand or know how the investor thinks, such as the financial analysis required to be an investor. They do, however, need the operators to have sound PE financial literacy skills and know how the PE partners look at their operations from a financial reporting standpoint. With PE financial literacy, the expectation is that operators know how PE firms measure progress and momentum. Some operators may be coming from a background where they never needed to make financial budgets, and they may not even know how that process works. In this business phase, though, the PE partner expects the business to deliver on committed results every month, quarter, and year. Before we conclude, consider the following case study.

CASE STUDY
Nigel Travis–Former CEO of Dunkin' Brands

Before Dunkin' Brands—the parent company of Dunkin' Donuts—formed, there was Industrial Luncheon Services, a company founded in 1946 by William Rosenberg in Boston, Massachusetts. At the time, the business sold food to a customer base of predominantly factory workers. Over time, the business attained unprecedented success while also discovering that a large proportion of the sales was driven by two of their main product categories: coffee and doughnuts. This led Rosenberg to launch a coffee and doughnut shop named Open Kettle in 1948. Back then, they only charged five cents per doughnut and ten cents for each cup of coffee. From establishment onward, the company enjoyed several years of growing its customer base, which led the business to start franchising in 1955, leading to one hundred franchisees by 1963. By 2002, the company had over five thousand Dunkin' Donuts outlets in forty countries, making it a leader in its fast-food niche of coffee and doughnuts.[74]

The company was acquired multiple times, including in 2006, at a time when the company's growth had slowed down. Then, it was acquired for $2.4 billion by Bain Capital, The Carlyle Group, and Thomas H. Lee—three PE firms.[75] Adjusting the company's strategy and business model helped breathe new life into the business and led to the company ultimately going public in 2011 with a valuation that was double its original investment value.[76]

From 2009, Nigel Travis, an executive who had worked at Blockbuster, Burger King, and Papa John's, took the helm of Dunkin' Brands as CEO.[77] During his tenure at Dunkin' Brands from 2009 to 2018, Travis not only led the enterprise to great success,[78] he also helped take the company public

---

74   Rob Edelman, "Dunkin' Donuts," Encyclopedia.com, accessed October 1, 2025, https://www.encyclopedia.com/history/culture-magazines/dunkin-donuts.

75   "Inside Private Equity: A Case Study of Triumphs and Failures," Deloitte, November 6, 2024, https://www.deloitte.com/global/en/services/deloitte-private/research/family-office-insights-series-the-fireside.html.

76   Ibid.

77   Susan Adams, "Dunkin' Donuts Takes on the World: Leadership Lessons from the CEO," *Forbes*, October 1, 2013, https://www.forbes.com/sites/susanadams/2013/10/01/dunkin-donuts-takes-on-the-world-leadership-lessons-from-the-ceo/.

78   "Former Dunkin' CEO Nigel Travis: 'Challenge Everything,'" *Chief Executive*, accessed August 24, 2025, https://chiefexecutive.net/former-dunkin-ceo-nigel-travis-challenge-everything/.

and spearheaded global expansion into his native England, parts of the US, and various locations worldwide.[79]

In a 2013 interview with *Forbes*, Travis reflected on his transition from an HR background to corporate leadership roles, starting with Burger King. Upon being asked if he wanted to take on corporate leadership roles, he said the following:

> *We bought Burger King and I went to the company as head of human resources. After doing that for two years my boss said, "You have to run something." He sent me back to Europe. I ran Europe, the Middle East and Africa for Burger King. At the time I didn't know one end of a balance sheet from another. But my people skills got me through. The lesson there was, don't be afraid to say what you don't know and don't be frightened to be ignorant about something.*
>
> *The company took a helluva risk on me. I hadn't done an MBA. I hadn't done strategic planning. I had to learn all the accounting mumbo jumbo from my head of finance. Even marketing, I had to pick up as I went.[80]*

Are there any financial knowledge gaps that you have? Are you willing to "not be afraid to say what you don't know" and to start working on filling that gap the best way you can?

---

79 "Nigel Travis," Abercrombie & Fitch Co., https://corporate.abercrombie.com/blog/leadership/nigel-travis/.

80 Adams, "Dunkin' Donuts Takes on the World."

How to Impact KPIs

Once you have a good understanding of the KPIs crucial to the success of your PE venture, you must also understand how you can impact those KPIs to maximize profitability. This understanding must be shared with everyone on the management team, not just the CEO, CFO, or lead finance personnel. That is because the operational daily work may impact KPIs. A firm grasp of how those daily activities drive the numbers is vital. This means that the executive management team must not just depend on how these numbers are interpreted to them through reports but, rather, get an intimate grasp of the numbers. It is insufficient for the operator to accept these KPIs at face value, without observing the trail of these numbers from its daily source. Whether any member of the executive management team is aware of it or not, they are impacting the results. That is, regardless of whether or not those results are positive.

Consider the KPIs metrics—the numbers—as a function of activities or functions of work happening in the business. If necessary and possible, the CFO may need to educate other management members on which metrics impact the venture the most and therefore require the most attention. Before we discuss the PE perspective, let us consider the following case study.

CASE STUDY

"You Can't Make Bad Numbers Look Good"

Years ago, when I worked at another firm, the CEO of the company made a statement that had a profound impact on me. During an important top management meeting, a colleague made a dazzling presentation that left an indelible impression on me—though not in the way one might first assume.

This colleague had put in a great deal of energy and effort to make the presentation visually captivating with slick graphic design. He was also an exceptionally gifted orator who spoke with a confident tone and optimistic outlook. His presentation would have won me over if it were not for one matter that the CEO aptly highlighted once my colleague completed his presentation.

The CEO said to my colleague, "You can make a presentation as pretty and as optimistic as you want. But at the end of the day, your numbers still suck. And you can't make bad numbers look good."

I concur with the CEO.

At the end of the day, you must ask yourself, did you deliver or not? Did you offer significantly more substance than style?

CONCLUSION

In this chapter, we discussed the old and new financial metrics relevant to your business. Finances are the lifeblood of any business venture, including PE enterprises. It is crucial, therefore, that operators attain PE financial literacy skills and a common understanding with PE partners. The health of the business relationship and the success of the venture depend on it. In the next chapter, we will address the workforce dynamic.

KEY TAKEAWAYS

- Regardless of how you acquire PE financial literacy skills—whether through courses, mentorship, or other means—you must acquire these skills to be a successful operator.

- Operating with PE financial literacy as your foundational understanding not only helps you speak the same language as your PE partners but also allows you to work together in alignment.

CHAPTER 4

YOUR TEAM MAY NEED AN UPGRADE

—

The only thing worse than training your employees and having them leave is not training them and having them stay.[81]

—HENRY FORD

In chapter 3, we turned our attention to mastering PE financial language. In this chapter, we shift our attention toward upgrading your team. For many CEOs and founders who have come a long way with loyal teams, this can be a daunting task. This is particularly the case when CEOs realize that some employees and the company are no longer successfully aligned for the growth and longevity of the business. Outgrowing people is a common scenario; people who were right for the early phases of a company are no longer a good fit as the company enters growth and stabilization phases.

---

81   Tomas Chamorro-Premuzic, Seymour Adler, and Robert B. Kaiser, "What Science Says About Identifying High-Potential Employees," *Harvard Business Review*, October 3, 2017, https://hbr.org/2017/10/what-science-says-about-identifying-high-potential-employees.

As such, it is imperative for the business's leadership to be objective about the continued suitability of personnel, as failing to do so has the potential consequence of business failure. It is not just about meeting targets or profits. The business itself might fail if the wrong people are on board. In some cases, the business may survive with the wrong people, but it will not reach its full potential. To illustrate this point, let us consider the following case study.

CASE STUDY
Tesla's Origin Story

Before Elon Musk became the face of Tesla, there were Martin Eberhard and Marc Tarpenning. These two American engineers founded Tesla in a small office in 2003 with the idea of solving the problem of sustainability—in this case, where energy and transportation intercept. As such, they started an electric car company. Their vision was for an electric car that most people could afford, but they had two major problems.[82] First, though they were both engineers, they were not automotive engineers and, therefore, did not know how to make electric cars. Second, they did not have the capacity to hire a whole team to make the dream come true from scratch.[83] So, what could they do? They opted to partner with Lotus, a car manufacturing company, and hired several Lotus engineers. Eberhard also invested

---

82 Deanna Rampton, "The Story of Building Tesla, with Marc Tarpenning of Tesla and Shehnaz Daver of GV," Startup Grind, September 25, 2017, https://www.startupgrind.com/blog/the-story-of-building-tesla-with-marc-tarpenning-of-tesla-and-shernaz-daver-of-gv/.

83 Kim Java, host, "Tesla's Forgotten Founder Speaks Out – Exclusive w/ Martin Eberhard," August 28, 2024, YouTube, https://www.youtube.com/watch?v=88KHfX_kPIY.

$100,000 in AC Propulsion, a struggling car manufacturing startup that had made three prototypes up to that point. He also paid the company to build a car for him from spare parts it still had. Ultimately, they ended up customizing one of the existing three prototypes and used that to woo potential investors with test-drives.[84] Fortunately, their efforts to gain investments paid off. Some of the investors they courted, the most prominent being Musk, ended up investing. Musk alone invested more than $30 million and became the chairman of the company's board.[85]

Once investments poured in, the business had a real chance of not only surviving but truly thriving. Yet, as with most businesses, it was not all just smooth sailing. There were challenges along the way, particularly between Eberhard (who was CEO at the time) and the board. Budget overruns, schedule delays, and differences with Musk (one of the main investors) were among the most pressing challenges. One particular bone of contention was the risk factor. Eberhard felt that some board-level decisions increased risk and cost, such as switching from a composite material (used by Lotus) to carbon fiber for the car's body. These conflicts ultimately led to Eberhard being pushed out of the company.[86]

Fast-forward to the present. Tesla has contributed to Musk's outstanding financial success. It has led to not only

---

84   Ibid.

85   Barbara A. Schreiber, "Martin Eberhard and Marc Tarpenning," Britannica Money, May 16, 2024, accessed September 28, 2024, https://www.britannica.com/money/ Martin-Eberhard-and-Marc-Tarpenning.

86   Ibid.

making Musk a billionaire with a net worth of $371 billion but also making him the richest man in the world—as of the time of writing in 2025.[87]

Eberhard acknowledged that Tesla's ongoing leadership achieved indisputable financial success, regardless of the difference in vision he had with the board—particularly Musk. He stated, "He's done amazing, right? The company is huge. He became the richest man in the world from it. I can't criticize too much ..."[88]

When Eberhard was asked if it was hard to give up control, he responded, "Yes and no. I didn't start this company as a get-rich-quick scheme. It was insane at the time to start a car company ... To see that succeed, especially not just that we started a car company, but we started a revolution. All the car companies in the world now make electric cars because of this car. Yeah. So that I'm quite happy about that ..."[89]

Look at the graciousness with which the early founders of Tesla handled letting go of their business to leadership. Are you prepared to embrace the new vision that PE investment may herald? Do you accept that realizing this new vision may mean making some leadership changes?

---

87   Dan Moskowitz, "The 10 Richest People in the World," Investopedia, last updated November 1, 2025, https://www.investopedia.com/articles/investing/012715/5-richest-people-world.asp.

88   Java, "Tesla's Forgotten Founder Speaks Out."

89   Ibid.

As in the Tesla scenario, PE firms push for leadership changes, typically when performance requirements are not being met or if there is a significant cultural mismatch. Sometimes, PE firms can see these challenges well in advance and may make those talent upgrades even before the deal closes. However, it does take time to evaluate the performance of the business and the style of the leadership team. As such, the exact efforts you make in upgrading your team are situational.

In the Tesla case study, it is easy to see the enormous financial and growth benefits that the new leadership brought to the team. As stated, an objective determination is needed to identify the individuals that are a good fit for your business.

Consider the following case study.

CASE STUDY
Old Brown Dog Veterinary Partners

It is not uncommon to finish college and join your family's business after graduation. What is uncommon, though, is to graduate from college, work at a PE firm for several months, and then unify two of your family's businesses. Yet, that is what Dr. Joseph Marchell accomplished.[90]

Marchell had grown up with both of his parents, each a veterinarian with their own individual veterinary practice. With their passion for caring for animals, he followed in their footsteps but with one big difference: He had an interest in PE. So, once he had graduated—broke, and saddled with debt—he took a job in PE for six months. During this time,

---

90   "Case Study 76: Veterinary Mini Roll-Up," Apex Business Advisors, accessed November 10, 2025, https://www.kcapex.com/case-study-76-veterinary-mini-roll-up/.

he learned how to make a more prosperous veterinary business. He was aware that most practitioners centered their efforts on their patients—the animals. However, this also meant not as much attention was paid to the financial matters of the business. Marchell noted growth in the valuation of businesses in his field and realized that there was significant potential if the businesses were consolidated in a tactical roll-up. When he pitched this to his parents, they were open to his proposal.[91]

In 2020, Old Brown Dog Veterinary Partners (OBDVP) was born. This was the tactical roll-up of three businesses: each of Marchell's parents' veterinary practices and an additional one. These businesses were acquired at ten times EBITDA. In just under two years, they ran such an efficient outfit that they were able to exit at roughly three times the purchase price of the venture.[92]

Some of the key talent-related changes Marchell made that allowed their business massive success were as follows:

Because he took the time to bring in a professional operations manager and someone fully in charge of HR, Old Brown Dog started seeing more profitability right away, leading to an even better possible multiple of EBITDA.

Further, Joseph was ultimately de-risking all these practices by putting people in place that reduced the key man burden on the practicing vet. Indeed, once all those functions had been hired, even the vet himself

---

91   Ibid.

92   "A Behind-the-Scenes Look at a Mini Rollup," *Built to Sell*, November 4, 2022, https://builttosell.com/radio/episode-362/.

could leave, and the practice could continue on with a new doctor. The mom-and-pop one-off practices were becoming part of a well-oiled machine.

With the experience in PE that Marchell had before forming OBDVP, he attempted to handle the M&A role of the business while also working as a veterinarian in the company. However, he quickly realized he was completely out of his depth and hired an M&A advisor. The M&A advisor began by undoing some of what Marchell had done to right the ship, starting with taking the business off the market. Then, he ended discussions with potential buyers to ensure changes to EBITDA were clarified and a more profitable narrative was generated.[93]

What were the results of all these efforts? Twenty-two interested buyers, leading to eight letters of interest. From there, Marchell selected the best three and requested their best offers. In the end, the business was sold at a value that his parents had never fathomed could be possible.[94]

Without these changes to the talent of the business (i.e., hiring a professional operations manager, a lead HR professional, and later an M&A advisor), do you suppose they still would have enjoyed the same or similar success?

One crucial aspect of ensuring you have the best people for the job is to provide team members with the business's expectations and a clear understanding of quantitative business measures. The expectations should be a well-documented agreement and allow for the

---

93   Apex Business Advisors, "Case Study 76."

94   Ibid.

talent to sign off on them. In many ways, this agreement serves as a function of measurement, clearly presenting all stated objectives quantitatively. If, over the course of doing business, a person who signed the agreement does not meet expectations, you must understand why and what the factors are. Sometimes, there might be legitimate reasons for unmet expectations. Therefore, it is necessary to keep an open mind. However, after continual poor performance, it should be clear that the person is not a good fit for the business, and you then need to take the next steps to remedy the situation.

Importance of Assessing Talent

Regardless of whether your business has high-performing staff, you need to assess your staff's capabilities. Former owners often feel earnest loyalty to staff who have weathered the storms with them, regardless of their performance. To approach this scenario objectively and ensure expectations are understood and met, your business needs to urgently implement performance management systems and quantifiable business objectives.

As you professionalize the business, in some cases, you will need to swiftly make personnel changes. Fortunately, there are ways you can accomplish this compassionately and without loss of dignity for the affected staff members. If you reach the point of having to let a staff member go, then you must have gone through the process of reaching agreement on the company's measurable expectations. Therefore, when you sit face-to-face with them to have this discussion, that process alone already significantly and preemptively takes the emotion out of it. You then can share with them exactly where they did not get the work done or meet the stated objectives. This is also a time to express where they can make improvements, if any. While you are releasing them from your organization, this opportunity to share possible improvements they can make may help them in their next work engagement.

Over the years, I have found some good employees who simply no longer fit in the companies I led. These were people I would easily and happily recommend to my network for other work opportunities. From a standpoint of empathy, to ensure their success going forward, I felt compelled to offer them my perspective on their performance, even though it would no longer have a bearing on my business's success or failure. It is worth noting that these were individuals who had the right character and good work ethics. In some cases, these people could be trained and developed and might thrive in a different role. However, in the case of individuals whose behavior was problematic for the organization or who were culturally misaligned with it, the complexities were irreconcilable.

Letting go of a good human being who is simply not a good fit for the organization does not have to be an uncomfortable experience. Indeed, I would not only recommend them to my network for work opportunities by making a few calls and becoming a reference but, occasionally, would also connect the individual to a mentor who could help them build up their skills. This was an offer many outgoing employees appreciated. In other cases, I offered the individuals books and other tangible educational materials to utilize for their personal development.

How to Upgrade the Team

With the time constraints imposed on your business investment by the holding period of PE ventures, any upgrades to your team must be carried out expeditiously. The goal is that the business starts to perform at a high level quickly to ensure value creation and overall favorable business outcomes.

Due to the nature of PE businesses, your recruiting strategies will have to change for optimal success. Ideally, you will onboard some personnel with previous PE experience. Those are the individuals who will easily fit into the emerging business culture and the pace of transformation that the business is undergoing and who also have a working knowledge of the PE playbook. Hands-on operators who can roll up their sleeves and get involved in driving performance are usually preferred over the strategic, visionary type of operators.

Performance-based compensation should be implemented in a straightforward manner. Most importantly, this means ensuring performance metrics are clearly defined and articulated. The most successful way of accomplishing this is to ensure that you have discussed and agreed upon these performance metrics as a group beforehand. Thereafter, relevant parties assessing the results should be aware that the results of these metrics are not up for debate or simply mere suggestions. They are, in fact, what the business is depending on to achieve a successful outcome.

Strategies that capitalize on the nature of PE ventures being fast-paced and responsive to individual contribution may help attract recruits that fit the culture and PE dynamics. To make your business even more alluring for great talent, structuring attractive compensation plans and equity options may assist it in garnering the attention of top performers.

Evaluating Talent

PE firms evaluate existing talent over time, once the PE executive has had time to assess the executive's leadership capabilities and the business's performance. Steady, strong performance, combined with high character, usually leads to long-term opportunities with PE firms. Operators desiring to retain their roles or move up the ladder should focus their attention on cultivating positive relational attributes and commendable performance.

One beneficial approach you can adopt is that of Reid Hoffman (co-founder of LinkedIn) and his colleagues. The approach considers the relationship between you—the leader—and the employee as an alliance over and above anything else. This alliance transcends the work dynamic you have now and operates with the understanding that this working relationship is temporary. The approach involves three aspects: implementing recruitment based on "tours of duty" with express expectations, facilitating the establishment of external employee networks, and orchestrating the development of active alumni networks that are sustained throughout the careers of employees.[95] Here is an example of how Hoffman employed the concept of tours of duty:

> *When Reid founded LinkedIn, he set the initial employee compact as a four-year tour of duty, with a discussion at two years. If an employee moved the needle on the business during the four years, the company would help advance his career. Ideally this would entail another tour of duty at the company, but it could also mean a position elsewhere.*[96]

The tours of duty concept not only encourages productive work ethics but also helps build a network of passionate advocates for you and your business. The employee makes significant career gains that

---

95 Reid Hoffman, Ben Casnocha, and Chris Yeh, "Tours of Duty: The New Employer-Employee Compact," *Harvard Business Review*, June 2013, https://hbr.org/2013/06/tours-of-duty-the-new-employer-employee-compact.

96 Ibid.

benefit them beyond their paychecks, and all of this cultivates mutual trust and loyalty between both parties.[97]

With PE ventures, the talent you need in the fix stage is not necessarily the talent your business needs for the long term. Similarly, the growth or expansion stages bring with them unique challenges that require specialists who are expertly trained to navigate those challenges.

As businesses become more structured and the expectations change, it is often the case that more experience and know-how are required to achieve the desired outcome. It is not unusual for a business to outgrow the capabilities of many of the executives in the organization. What got the business to point A may be very different from what's required to get to point B or C. Furthermore, parting ways does not have to be a negative or detrimental experience for employees. Rather, it can be a steppingstone to upward career mobility for outgoing staff who are ushered on to the next role in their careers. Lastly, the team evaluation is not a onetime exercise. Rather, it is an exercise that is conducted regularly, particularly by the PE partners, to ensure the business stays on track.

CONCLUSION

In this chapter, we zeroed in on the necessity of a high-performing team and the task of upgrading your team if you have irreconcilable performance gaps. In the next chapter, we will shift our attention to your board and how you can advocate with them.

---

97   Ibid.

KEY TAKEAWAYS

- Be extremely objective because of the potential consequences of failure.
- Be honest with yourself when someone isn't suitable for the team.
- Provide team members with the expectations and quantitative business measures.
- Ensure all relevant parties sign off on the agreement.

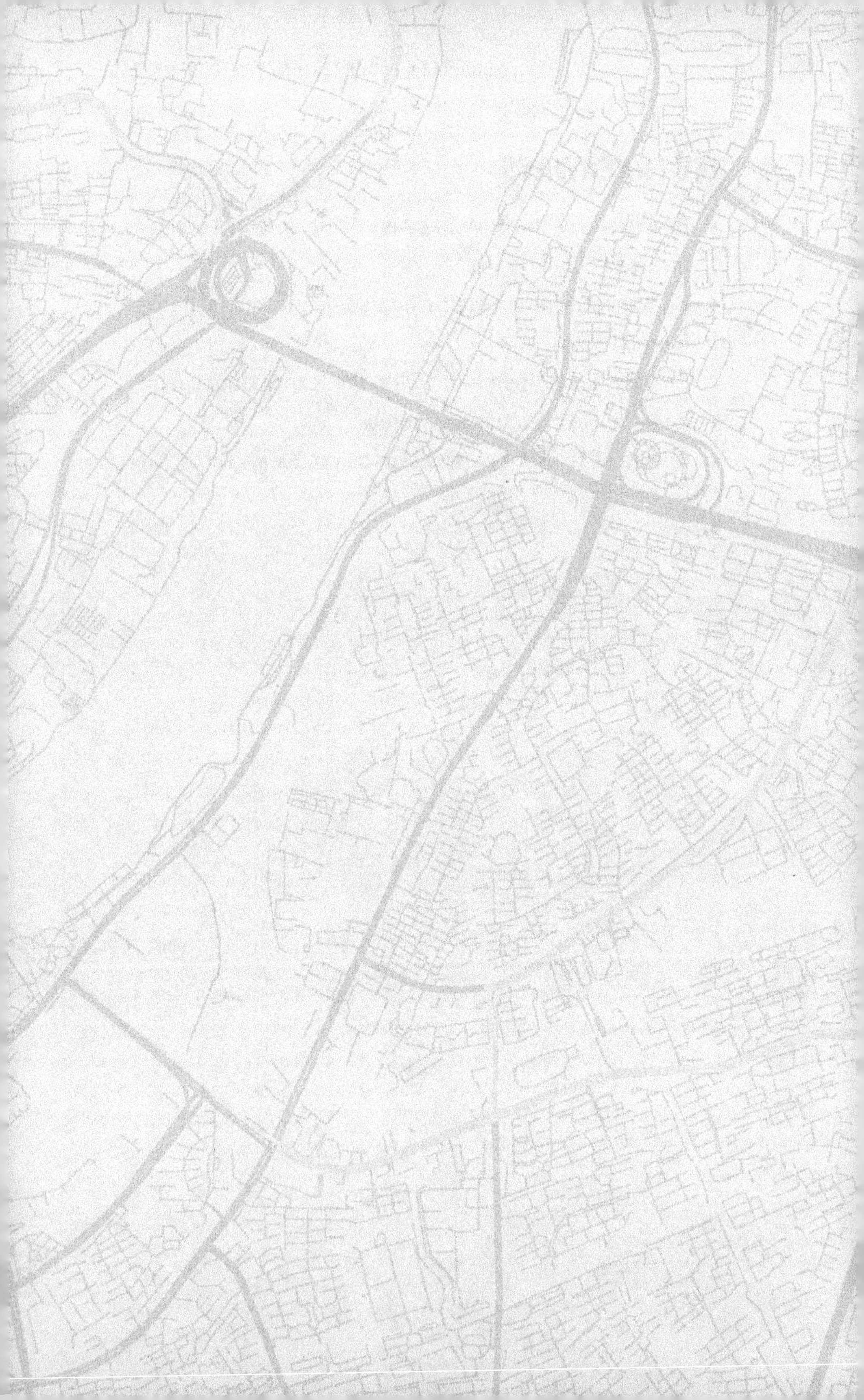

CHAPTER 5

ADVOCATING WITH YOUR BOARD

The very essence of leadership is that you have to have a vision. It's got to be a vision you articulate clearly and forcefully on every occasion. You can't blow an uncertain trumpet.[98]

—REVEREND THEODORE HESBURGH

Ensuring you have the right people in your company is vital, as we covered in the previous chapter. However, they are not the only people whose expertise your business success depends on. Your company's board is another group of people whose efforts directly impact the success or failure of your business. In this chapter, we address matters to do with advocating with your company's board. These matters include board dynamics, best practices for board meetings, and managing your relationship with individual board members.

Your company's board of directors is responsible for your business and strategically oversees it, as articulated in your company's

---

98   Kevin Kruse, "100 Best Quotes on Leadership," *Forbes*, October 16, 2012, https://www.forbes.com/sites/kevinkruse/2012/10/16/quotes-on-leadership/.

articles of incorporation and corporate bylaws.[99] As such, the board's structure and dynamics are simply functions of the business, and there is no exact structure that it must follow, because it is situational. If it complies with the company's articles of incorporation and corporate bylaws, the board can be just the PE partners or a mix of the company's CEO, operating partners, PE investors, and other parties.

Unlike in a public company, you will have many opportunities to engage or collaborate with your board. In a public company, you typically don't talk to your board until there's a quarterly meeting. In PE, you may even talk to them every day. Advocating is about developing a relationship with all the parties until there's alignment. It is, therefore, a constant process of developing connectivity with board members. As in any other case, people leave, and the business adapts because the structure is designed to be fluid.

CASE STUDY
Conflicts of Interest and Professionalism

Over a decade ago, I was part of a new management team for a global business that was tasked with the responsibility of spearheading a turnaround. Along with hiring me—as president—and other top management professionals, an interim CEO was appointed who also happened to occupy the role of chairman of the company. To be clear, as the chairman, his role was that of an independent board member, not an investor or part of the PE firm.

---

99   James Chen, "Board of Directors: Definition and Role," Investopedia, last updated May 20, 2025, https://www.investopedia.com/terms/b/boardofdirectors.asp.

In time, my colleagues on the management team started to notice that the chairman/CEO tried to develop personal friendships with board members. We noted him taking some board members out for private dinners—and, on one occasion, skiing. This was all on the company's dime. You could argue that maybe his method was a soft approach toward fostering goodwill and advocating for what the business needed to get back on track. That was not the case; it was evident to us that his agenda was self-serving. He was attempting to line up additional board jobs or future opportunities with the PE firm. Furthermore, the time and energy he spent ingratiating himself with the board exceeded that which he spent steering the company. He hardly attended management meetings and rarely engaged with the management team. He also had to commute quite some distance, and he was often not in the office. This led to the management team growing exceedingly frustrated, so much so that, eventually, we had enough. We ultimately informed the board of all our grievances about the CEO's lack of decorum, how it was impacting the business, and our willingness to collectively quit if someone who would champion our interests was not appointed.

To our surprise, the board members had no idea of the dynamics we informed them of. Up to that point in time, their interactions with the interim CEO had led them to believe that all these efforts somehow implied a level of commitment to the business. Thankfully, the board took our concerns seriously and took swift action. They removed the individual from the interim CEO role and

> eventually also from the role of chairman of the board. Fortunately, the CEO who was hired after him did a commendable job of representing the business and the team and maintaining a professional distance from the PE firm.

Board Dynamics

A PE venture's board is typically composed of the deal team, operating partners, and, in some cases, outside executives who have relevant experience. When it comes to actual board meetings, PE boards generally anticipate presentations (such as via PowerPoint) or other materials. These materials may contain visual components, such as charts, graphs, and graphics. They should assist you in articulating where the business is in terms of performance, how the business arrived there, where it's going, and how it will get there.

When it comes to the board making decisions, board members collaborate among themselves and with the company's executive leadership. The circumstances surrounding the decision usually inform when and to what degree the management team is involved in the actual decision.

To arrive at win–win scenarios from board meetings, you need to develop a rapport and sustain healthy working relationships with the deal team members and operating partners. Over time, you will understand what the business communication style might be and when and how to engage your PE partners. The ideal dynamic to create with the PE team is one of mutual respect and trust. You can earn this respect and trust by exhibiting successful conflict management, executing difficult decisions, demonstrating strong character, and ensuring sustained high performance.

Rite Way Heating, Cooling & Plumbing's story, in the following case study, is a shining example of successful advocacy with the board.

CASE STUDY
Rite Way Heating, Cooling & Plumbing

PE firms have generated outstanding profitability from ventures in the home services industry in areas such as HVAC, plumbing, and electrical. Since 2022, PE firms have acquired approximately eight hundred of these companies in the US. The level of success in this type of business has been so widespread that pundits have said that skillful entrepreneurs in these trades do not need to think of Silicon Valley to have hopes of joining America's millionaire class. One article on the subject highlighted this phenomenon accordingly:[100]

> *Private equity, however, is no foreign player in the skilled trades these days. PE firms across the country have been scooping up home services like HVAC—that is, heating, ventilation and air conditioning—as well as plumbing and electrical companies. They hope to profit by running larger, more profitable operations. Their growth marks a major shift, taking home-services firms away from family operators by offering mom-and-pop shops seven-figure and eight-figure paydays. It is a contrast from previous*

---

100 "ICYMI: WSJ Highlights How Private Equity Transforms Plumbing and HVAC Small Businesses, Boosting Wages and Growth," American Investment Council, October 15, 2024, https://www.investmentcouncil.org/icymi-wsj-highlights-how-private-equity-transforms-plumbing-and-hvac-small-businesses-boosting-wages-and-growth/.

generations, when more owners handed companies down to their children or employees.

The wave of investment is minting a new class of millionaires across the country, one that small business owners say is helping add more shine to working with a tool belt. Private-equity investors have purchased nearly 800 HVAC, plumbing and electrical companies since 2022, according to data from PitchBook. And those are just the biggest deals—plenty of smaller-scale purchases aren't tracked, and sellers are reluctant to share exact details about their PE payouts.[101]

One good example of this is Rite Way Heating, Cooling & Plumbing. With its origins in Tuscon, Rite Way was founded in 1959 and offers heating, cooling, plumbing, and electrical services. At the time the business was acquired by a PE-backed business, the company's revenue stood at $30 million. By 2024, the company's revenue had increased by roughly $40 million, to approximately $70 million.

The financial injection from PE allowed the company resources to invest in expansion—adding vehicles to the fleet, hiring more personnel, and establishing and running technician training and apprenticeship projects. Some of the direct advantages of the expansion, particularly the fleet of vehicles, were faster response times and better wages for the staff. According to one investment firm, the

---

101 "Private Equity Is Pouring Money into Skilled-Trade Small Businesses: Excerpts from *The Wall Street Journal*," MultiBriefs, October 2024, https://multibriefs.com/briefs/ cema/Privateequity.pdf. Originally published as Te-Ping Chen, "America's New Millionaire Class: Plumbers and HVAC Entrepreneurs," *Wall Street Journal*, October 12, 2024.

average pay increase for technicians stands at 20 percent in the first post-acquisition—that's with wages, bonuses, and commission combined.[102] By 2021, the company had garnered over two thousand reviews on Google, a 4.9-star rating, and an A+ Better Business Bureau rating. It is safe to say, its profitability is well-deserved all around.[103]

However, when it comes to understanding what happens behind the "board advocacy scenes," not much direct information is available. Public articles do imply compelling evidence that all parties share a healthy rapport, characterized by mutual trust and confidence. One telling sign is that once the business was acquired by PE investors, Rick Walter, the President of Rite Way as of 2024, did not immediately leave. Rather, he made two telling decisions. Firstly, he chose to retain a 25 percent stake in the business. Secondly, he accepted the role of president for some additional years, after which he intends to retire.

The fact that the PE firm offered him the opportunity to stay on as president for some more years is a prime indicator that they had established a healthy rapport, beyond him being an effective leader for the business. Furthermore, Walter keeping a 25 percent stake in the business and accepting the extended work opportunity imply that these positive sentiments may have been mutual.

---

102 "About Rite Way," Rite Way Heating, Cooling & Plumbing, accessed November 5, 2025, https://ritewayac.com/about-riteway/.

103 "Redwood Services Announces Strategic Partnership with Rite Way," *HVAC & Refrigeration Insider Online*, March 29, 2021, https://hvacinsider.com/redwood-services-announces-strategic-partnership-with-rite-way/.

> Each party said it best in a news announcement. The CEO of Redwood Services, Richard Lewis, stated, "We are honored to have the opportunity to help Rite Way achieve the next chapter of growth, while protecting the company's rich culture, brand and legacy ... From our first conversations with Rick and his team, we were impressed with the culture, 60+ year track record in the Tucson marketplace, shared passion for people and focus on customer service. We picked a great partner in Rite Way and look forward to supporting the entire team under the leadership of Rick and General Manager Chris Sundin."[104]

> Walter's response echoed similar sentiments: "We're excited to partner with Redwood Services on a collective vision of growing Rite Way ... Redwood's recognition and support of our people-focused culture is a driving difference that makes this partnership a great fit for us. Our employees, customers and the Tucson community will benefit from an even stronger operational framework which will allow us to continue to provide the best services and equipment."[105]

The outcome of this partnership speaks for itself, far beyond words. We may be right to assume that this partnership was not only profitable but also harmonious. As you know, this is not always the case.

---

104 Ibid.

105 Ibid.

Best Practices

When it comes to developing and maintaining a healthy relationship with the board, two overarching approaches are necessary. These are preparation and proactivity.

PREPARATION

You would likely agree that preparedness for important meetings is a reasonable expectation. Effective preparation includes anticipating the main issues that will be discussed and preparing discussion items to help make important points. Anticipate what the questions are going to be and cover all bases so that there are no surprises for you during these meetings. What you do not want during these meetings are questions from the board such as "Where is this coming from?" and "Why didn't we know about this before?"

When appropriate and necessary, ensure you accompany your discussion points with visual aids. During these meetings, you can request assistance from the board when you feel their support can be helpful. Regardless, most boards tend to ask how they can be of help.

There are essentially three main purposes of a board meeting. You may need a formal forum to inform the board members of matters requiring their attention and to update them on the performance of the company. On other occasions, you may need to gain support or buy-in from the board on new initiatives. Lastly, you may intend for the board meeting to be a means of acquiring resources (financial and human). Typically, boards are quite constructive and try to find ways to support the company's objectives, such as identifying individuals or third parties with valuable know-how or connections.

If we take a closer look at the third purpose of board meetings— as a strategic resource—we must ensure proper management of the flow of information between both parties for it to be successful. This flow of information can be either formal or informal. Outside the board meeting, there will be many opportunities to keep the board informed as to the progress of the business. Your business may opt to do what many PE firms do, which is to hold weekly calls with the CEO or have direct access to the financial performance of the business. This approach ensures you have opportunities to express what you need, and hopefully obtain it swiftly.

One helpful habit I developed in my experiences with boards is to have a meeting with the deal leader in advance of the actual board meeting. In that meeting, typically a week before the board meeting, I probe the deal lead for any information that may help me adequately prepare. By covering what I need to prepare for in advance, we avoid any unnecessary surprises.

Alongside adequate preparation, being proactive is a must. You must take a level of responsibility for or even ownership of the board agenda and board relationship. Often, we see two types of CEOs. One type manages their board effectively, and the other does not. The first type of CEO thinks about the agenda, ensures topics are relevant, handles big issues in advance, and strives to ensure that there are never any surprises. This type of CEO does not merely operate this way because of sheer experience. Rather, they can command such efforts because of how comfortable they are in their role and in their leadership abilities.

CEOs who do not exercise sufficient responsibility over their relationship with their board are ineffective and, as a result, reactive. Reactivity is not helpful for anyone and often leads to frustration all around. The CEO experiences frustration because of the number of inquiries made by the board and the interference that they cause. The board experiences frustration because the CEO does not own their part of board interactions. You must realize that your role as CEO is to own and manage the board process. This may be new to you, but I assure you, this is what the best CEOs do.

Managing Your Relationships with the Board

Engaging your board is not limited to these regular board meetings. In fact, to be effective, you must do more than this. You must work at fostering healthy working relationships with your company's board members. This extends to the times when you interact with them between board meetings. Individual board members have certain styles, preferred concerns, or functional areas that they have a specific interest in. Over time, the style and idiosyncrasies of board members become apparent, and you can anticipate what may be of interest to them. Those meetings you arrange prior to board meetings with the deal lead or operating partner can help you in your efforts to cultivate a positive working relationship.

As with all relationships, disagreements are inevitable. In such cases, you may think it is ideal to state your opinion that happens to be counter to what the board wants. When pushing back is necessary, it should be because there is a real belief that what you are advocating is in the best interest of the business. It should not be ego-based or performative. Rather, it should be out of concern that the business will suffer an adverse impact.

CONCLUSION

In this chapter, we addressed the need for advocacy with your board. In the next chapter, we will turn our attention to the challenges that you will navigate during the M&A process.

KEY TAKEAWAYS

- Anticipate the key questions, and utilize visual aids to help make your key points in preparation for board discussions.
- Advocating is about developing a relationship with all the parties until there's alignment.
- When pushing back is necessary, it should be because there is a real belief that what you are advocating is in the best interest of the business, not because of ego.

CHAPTER 6

THE M&A CHANGE

—

Change is the law of life and those who look only to the past or present are certain to miss the future.[106]

–PRESIDENT JOHN F. KENNEDY

As mentioned earlier, your company can grow organically or inorganically through M&A. In the previous chapter, we focused our attention on how you can conduct effective advocacy with your company's board. In this chapter, we will discuss the avenue of inorganic growth that you can attain through M&A. People management, common integration challenges, and the management of customer relations are among the areas of M&A-related change that will be discussed. Growing through acquisition is a popular strategy, though it is not the only way. Still, there are many firms that focus on growing through this strategy. You will need to familiarize yourself with how to function at a fast pace and how to build a strategic approach to M&A.

---

106 "50 Personal Growth Quotes to Inspire Your Journey," Southern New Hampshire University, August 8, 2022, https://www.snhu.edu/about-us/newsroom/education/personal-growth-quotes.

Running a business is intensive, and so is conducting M&A-related activities in tandem. You can't trade off your time or focus. You must be able to invest in acquiring businesses while the core business continues to perform. Time management and resource allocation become important when you are buying businesses and operating the company.

The PE partners are typically very involved in the acquisition process. In my experience, many on the investment side of PE have investment banking backgrounds. Investment bankers typically manage the work associated with buying and selling companies for their clients. As such, it is not uncommon to have very active participation from your PE partners in acquisitions, given this experience set.

CASE STUDY
The Silent-Quitting CEO

Taking a back seat in a business you founded and committed your life to is not easy. However, that's the predicament many founders find themselves in when they successfully obtain PE investment. And this is the circumstance that Bob, a middle-aged founder of a commercial building products company, found himself in several years ago. At the time, I was the CEO of the platform company, and Bob was the founder of one of the companies we had acquired during our company's growth phase. We offered him the opportunity to stay on as part of the leadership of his company after we bought it. He accepted.

However, this meant that Bob was no longer the top boss. This was not something Bob was used to. Neither was it something that had adequately sunk into the hearts and minds of the employees who had been loyal to him and were still with the company.

You see, Bob was affable and well-liked—the kind of gentleman everyone earnestly calls a great guy, because they are. We saw no matters of grave concern prior to signing all the paperwork and adding him to our pool of talent. The challenges we experienced presented themselves after a while.

The challenge was that, though Bob had willingly sold his business to ours, over time, it seemed that he harbored some level of resentment for doing so. Although he had millions of dollars in the bank from selling the business to us, he started creating friction in the business and contributing to growing discontent among the staff. This translated further into poor staff performance. I also tend to think that, for Bob, having millions of dollars in the bank was less important than his need for notoriety. All that the world could see was that he sold his company and had decided to stay on as an employee—albeit an important one. I tend to think that, at some level, Bob felt his significance in the organization decrease. This supposed downgrade in social hierarchy may have led him to demonstrate the level of internalized resistance that started showing up, culminating in him poisoning the proverbial well.

Naturally, when I noticed what was going on, I sat down with him and discussed the situation at great depth. By the end of that discussion, I hoped we would have smooth sailing. We did, to a degree, but not as expected. Bob went from vocal resistance to silent quitting.

> At this point, it was clear that it was time to inform the board of the problem and the possible solution. Once the board had been informed of Bob's conduct, they thoroughly understood and supported my decision to let Bob go when his lack of participation and involvement eventually reached a fever pitch. It is worth noting that at that point, his influence was so pervasive that almost half a dozen of his most loyal employees left with him. Thankfully, after the dust settled, the company's performance rebounded, and we were able to establish a performance-oriented culture.
>
> If you reflect on Bob's conduct, can you see what you would have done differently in his shoes?

Experience shows us that the best solution is to clearly explain, to all relevant stakeholders, the merits of the acquisition and how the business ultimately wins because of the implementation of new systems, processes, etc.

PE firms measure M&A success beyond financial metrics. Non-financial success factors are largely relegated to cultural fit. If you can answer the following questions in the affirmative, it is a good indication that the deal was successful beyond the financials:

- Does the acquired company buy into the new owner's strategy?
- Do the employees of the acquired company feel and act as part of the new company? You can identify the answer even through simple linguistic observation—for example, whether they use terms such as "us" or "them" in reference to the new dynamic.
- How engaged are the new employees, and are they excited to be a part of the new entity?

These are good indicators of a successful transaction. Beyond these questions, you can adopt a more methodical approach by using anonymous surveys and other informal communications to assert how good a fit the new company is.

Employee Management

You may note from the case study, and from M&A in general, that a significant part of navigating M&A successfully is people management. This skill is essential, especially in cases where platform companies absorb competing enterprises. For that reason, it is important to gain alignment on the virtues of the acquisition and how bringing the businesses together can potentially create more value than each business would have if they continued operating independently.

However, if you do buy a direct competitor, your job is to create harmony. All parties need to keep in mind that if the company is eventually purchased, someone representing each organization agreed to this acquisition or merger. Therefore, it is important for that person, or someone equally responsible, to explain to their team the rationale behind it. The goal here is to get buy-in from members of staff. So, if communicating this information is your responsibility, then you must figure out how to message it, typically with an optimistic and future-oriented perspective.

Whatever decision you need to make, particularly when it comes to employee management, swiftness is integral to success. You must make decisions fast and avoid dragging them out, especially when those decisions lead to necessary changes. Dragging out decision-making only slows down progress and makes it harder for the business to succeed. It may even jeopardize your ability to gain buy-in. Therefore, it is key to communicate your intentions and then follow through on them.

Business Management During M&A

Undergoing a merger or an acquisition is a very intensive exercise in and of itself. You need to successfully complete the integration of the new business into your platform business's operations while still running your core business. That calls for a level of balance that you need to plan for and brace yourself for when entering that stage.

The rule of thumb in any acquisition is, first, do no harm. Having a well-thought-out plan for when and how to best integrate the acquired business is critical for success. Acquirers need to think through seasonality. They also need to consider the capabilities of the talent within the business when considering the best time to begin the work of integrating. This calls for the establishment of clear milestones and ensuring that an individual or a dedicated team is accountable for the implementation of the work streams.

Managing Customer Relations

So far, we have discussed what you need to do to manage your employees and the business. We also need to discuss managing your customer relations.

The key here is to ensure that the customer experience is enhanced or, at the very least, does not deteriorate because of the acquisition. As stated, with employees, communicating to them the value of the acquisition is vital, and in some cases, it may also be necessary to communicate the acquisition and rationale to the customer base. It is up to your discretion and judgment to determine which customer groups need to be told and which details are important.

Key Development Opportunities While Leading M&A Initiatives

Many PE firms devote significant resources to the M&A process, assisting management teams in sourcing, diligence, and integration. If the strategy is to buy and build, this support from the PE firm can be critical. While conducting business as usual and the uniqueness of M&A processes, you stand the chance to benefit from some of these key development opportunities. Sourcing, due diligence, and integration management are key aspects of the M&A process that you can capitalize on as you lead M&A initiatives.

Sourcing

Sourcing is the activity of identifying the deals or businesses to buy. You have the option of choosing how you will conduct your sourcing. Will you use investment bankers, use cold calling, consult your colleagues in the industry, or engage in any other relevant networking activity? Fortunately, the PE firm is there to assist, if you require it.

Due Diligence

Diligence or due diligence is the actual work associated with evaluating the business you wish to acquire. This phase includes management presentations, site visits, quality of earnings financial analysis, and the overall verification that you are buying what you think you are buying.

The due diligence expectations for the CEO and leadership team in M&A processes depend on several factors, such as the PE firm, the size of the business, and the experience of the leadership team. Due diligence can largely or completely be handled by the management team or might be controlled by the PE firm.

The Process

First, you submit an IOI to the seller. This is a document indicating your interest, with all the necessary terms associated with the purchase of the business, such as the price, the compensation program for the executives, and the timeframe within which the business would be evaluated (e.g., forty-five days). This leads to a *management presentation* with the other party. Under the assumption that you may proceed, you are required to sign a nondisclosure agreement because of the intimate nature of this type of appraisal. When the management meeting occurs, it typically includes touring the facilities and reviewing other relevant aspects of the business to be acquired. Under the nondisclosure agreement, you may see the company's financial statements and other relevant documentation. If both parties want to proceed, you progress to the LOI. The LOI is an exclusive agreement between both parties to close the agreement. To use a nonbusiness comparison, it is akin to a couple agreeing to be exclusive, with the idea of getting married later. This LOI implies that the parties are not engaging in alternative discussions with a competing interest for the same business opportunity. It also implies that the PE firm has already approved the capital to buy the company. On some occasions, closing doesn't happen. That is like being given an engagement ring and never following through with a legally binding marriage and the accompanying marriage certificate.

However, if the deal is closed, then both parties agree on a date to close, followed by signing. This signing of documents includes officializing the close of this deal and changing the legal structure of the company. The name of the business might change, and so could the physical location of the company, among other changes. All in all, everything discussed in the diligence phase will start to take effect. On the successful closing of the deal, integration commences. With integration, execution begins.

Common Integration Challenges

As M&A processes are inherently complex, you will face challenges often. Some of the challenges will be specifically around cultural integration during the acquisition. These common challenges include lack of decorum, lack of experience, and pushback or denial.

To address a lack of decorum or overall professionalism, the business needs a handbook or code of conduct that clearly presents the business's guiding principles. Employees are expected to not just read the document but to sign it as well. This signifies and affirms that they are aware of and accept what the company expects of their behavior.

If you identify a lack of experience among the team members of the acquired company, you can easily resolve this through personnel development efforts. Identify the areas in which performance standards are not being met and provide comprehensive training to these employees to the extent that it is possible so that they become proficient in those areas. With technology, training options have become extensive and no longer must involve face-to-face, in-person meetings. Video training or training manuals may suffice in some cases.

As outlined in the case study early in this chapter, you may sometimes experience pushback from employees who may feel a level of displacement from the dynamics of the integration process. Pushback or denial may be anticipated in scenarios where former employees resent the lack of independence that accompanies PE ventures. This challenge may stem from any level in the business and occurs when people behave in a way that is combative because they no longer have a sense of autonomy.

Remedying the problem of pushback or denial is quite straightforward. First, ensure the leadership of the company has explained the rationale for the deal to each employee. Then, communicate the expectations for both their performance and their behavior. Finally, if this doesn't work, it is time to consider other options, such as transitioning or opting out the employee. It is essential to carry out this third option when you notice ongoing disruption from employees struggling to integrate, because their presence or conduct can be influential in the company. If these types of employees are on board with the integration, they can be champions supporting the process. However, because of their influence, if they are not on board, they can appear to be villains.

A lot, if not all, of these common integration challenges can be overcome by effective documentation. Developing a document that lays out the key steps to be taken, and the sequence of events is highly recommended. Firms and companies that have completed many acquisitions likely have developed a "plug and play" process; therefore, this documentation may already be available to you.

Due to the complexities of the M&A process, proper and diligent documentation cannot be underestimated. Here is an incident I recall that illustrates this matter further.

CASE STUDY
A Formidable Memory

Before I started my career in PE, I held several roles. One of those roles was head of sales for a technology company in the '90s. There, I worked with strategic partners and their own sales forces. In my capacity, I was able to leverage the sales force of each of the three strategic partners. Due to the company's strategic arrangements, all the sales forces reported to me.

One day, the CEO and our head of M&A flew to San Diego to a meeting to look at a business the company was interested in acquiring. When the CEO returned, he came to my office and informed me that, effective immediately, I was to oversee M&A.

Naturally, his decision caught me by surprise, as I had not anticipated this sudden development. So, I inquired as to what informed his directive. In a matter-of-fact manner, the CEO informed me that at this meeting that they attended, the M&A leader did not take any notes, did not ask any questions, and failed to even attempt to build a rapport with anyone on the other side of the table. When the CEO asked him where his notes were and what he was going to utilize in their absence, the M&A partner's response was, "Don't worry, I got it."

Having been told about this incident, I understood immediately why that M&A leader was no longer in charge. A short time later, I ended up becoming his boss. Sometime after that, we had to let him go and hired someone with more M&A experience to replace him. Since then, I have been involved in hundreds of M&A transactions.

What may surprise you is that, on paper, this former head of M&A had a strong background and was qualified to do the work. Perhaps what caused his downward spiral at the company was more about his ego and less about his competency in the field. Perhaps arrogance told him that he was the most experienced guy in the company. Maybe this is what caused him to just show up, unprepared for meetings, and attend without taking notes for future reference. Perhaps he relied too heavily on his talent, charisma, and ability to talk extemporaneously.

However, what I do know for sure is that the CEO was an ex–GE executive. He advanced in his career by applying simple but effective efforts, such as note-taking and proactive communication and engagement with other parties. It is quite possible that the former M&A partner may have had a photographic memory, but to the CEO, this approach did not bode well. With this being the first potential deal that they went to look at together, the CEO assessed that this approach simply would not work for him. Since business was (and still is) fast paced, he opted not to wait and see if this man's mind was as capable of retaining every crucial detail as the M&A leader seemed to imply.

Because of the complexities of M&A, it is only natural and prudent to sweat the details.

Common M&A Pitfalls

Other than common integration challenges, you may come across some M&A pitfalls during your PE experience. The common pitfalls include poor integration, poor evaluation, and paying too much money for a company. In the next chapter, we will take a focused look at integration and how you can achieve excellence, so here, we will turn our attention to the rest of these pitfalls.

INEFFECTIVE EVALUATIONS

Evaluation-related pitfalls are extremely common. They include poor evaluation of your management team, competitive dynamics, and, more broadly, the external environment. When it comes to poor evaluation of the management team, again, I would liken it to matrimony. In the early stages—the honeymoon period—both parties see things through the proverbial rose-colored glasses. You may realize that the management evaluation was subpar once you start noticing problems with the management team. This is typically after the novelty and excitement die down and the true personalities of the new management executives start to show. To illustrate ineffective evaluation of management, consider the following case study.

CASE STUDY
The Oblivious CEO

A while ago, I was on the leadership team of an organization that decided to fill the CEO post internally. The board members felt they had a great candidate and consequently unanimously backed him for the position. After all, it was clear that he was loyal and dedicated to the company, having served in various capacities for many years, though not at the highest level. Regardless of that, he got the job, and for the next six months, he proceeded to fail the people who hired him.

This CEO's failures were not a result of ignorance. He knew full well that the company had an approval or authority matrix that he needed to defer to for expenditures. He was aware that certain expenses exceeding a stated value required approval from the PE partners. Yet, despite multiple warnings, he opted to ignore that stipulation to obtain authorization for large expenses. From staying at the best hotels and eating at the best restaurants to first-class flights and living a lavish lifestyle, this CEO decided to live his best life on the PE's financial resources. However, in PE, that isn't going to work long-term. Despite him being coached and reminded that this was not acceptable behavior at this company, the behavior continued. This lasted for approximately six months before he and several of his colleagues were fired.

What I found particularly disturbing is that this CEO was hired at a time when the firm was struggling financially. He was aware that this behavior was not adding to the solution; yet, he did it anyway. However, his reaction when he was let go was something that I did not anticipate. The CEO was shocked. And I was shocked that he was shocked. It appeared that he had not grasped that his continuous disregard for our fiscal management concerns would lead to getting fired, the natural outcome of this scenario.

Upon reflection, it became clear to me that we failed to effectively evaluate this individual and the others that we ended up firing. All along, we believed that we had identified individuals with high character to work in and represent the organization. We were mistaken. What we had been focused on when we hired them for these management roles was performance. These individuals were star performers who, by merit of their service, should have been promoted. However, the character issues that came to light made us realize that merit was not enough. Professionalism and a duty of care were equally important but gravely lacking in these few individuals. As such, you can conduct all the personality tests your organization feels are necessary and ask all the requisite questions—which candidates might answer to your satisfaction. However, the actual experience of working with them will reveal who they really are. Therefore, when you've made the determination that you have the wrong person or the wrong team, I think it is critical that you act quickly to rectify the situation. That's the lesson. Once you've made the determination, it's not going to get better.

It is worth questioning yourself in your hiring decisions. Are the criteria you focus on for identifying good leaders sufficient? Have you accounted for the value of good character?

INFLATED VALUE OF SALE

In M&A, paying too much for a company is the cardinal sin. Unfortunately, it is all too common. To avoid this pitfall, you must have comparatives lined up. This means you need to study similar businesses with similar competencies. Assess what they sold for and other relevant factors. This is akin to what you would do if you decided to sell your residence. Finding out how much the house across the street sold for gives you valuable intel. It gives you an indication of what the market price is. With this information, and more like it, you can determine if there is an opportunity to structure the transaction in a manner that makes it more affordable.

To use the house-buying analogy, if you proceed to finance the purchase of a house, you must make a down payment. The parallel to that in PE is rollover equity. Rollover equity is part of the sale of the business that you can agree to ratify as ownership stake in the business. You assess if that rollover equity is an option, and if it is, how much it should be. For example, if you decide to sell your business for $10 million but agree to have rollover equity of $2 million, then that $2 million will remain in the business as an investment to grow the business. It will be counted toward the value of that business's shares owned by the platform company. Other than rollover equity, there is also the concept of earnouts. Earnout refers to the performance-related compensation that the seller of a business is eligible to receive if they hit certain performance criteria, assuming they stay in the business. If you, as the seller, meet those performance standards after an agreed-upon period, you are issued financial rewards for meeting those objectives. The primary purpose of rollover equity and earnouts is to help mitigate the risk associated with the value of the purchase.

CONCLUSION

Every PE venture desires growth, and organic, day-to-day growth is not the only option available to you. Inorganic growth through acquiring other businesses or merging with other businesses is a legitimate and time-tested option. In this chapter, we explored this option and aspects pertaining to it, including people and business management during M&A, common integration challenges that you may face due to M&A, and common pitfalls. In the next chapter, we will take a deeper look at *integration excellence*, a process required for your business when conducting M&A.

KEY TAKEAWAYS

- M&A is a viable and popular growth strategy that your company may wish to employ.
- Exceptional time management is required to navigate the M&A dynamics because of the strain on finite resources (such as time) that the process requires, in addition to whatever other daily business responsibilities you already have.
- Be honest. Never promise your staff members that nothing will change, as change is inevitable. Rather, be committed to helping them navigate any changes that may come along.

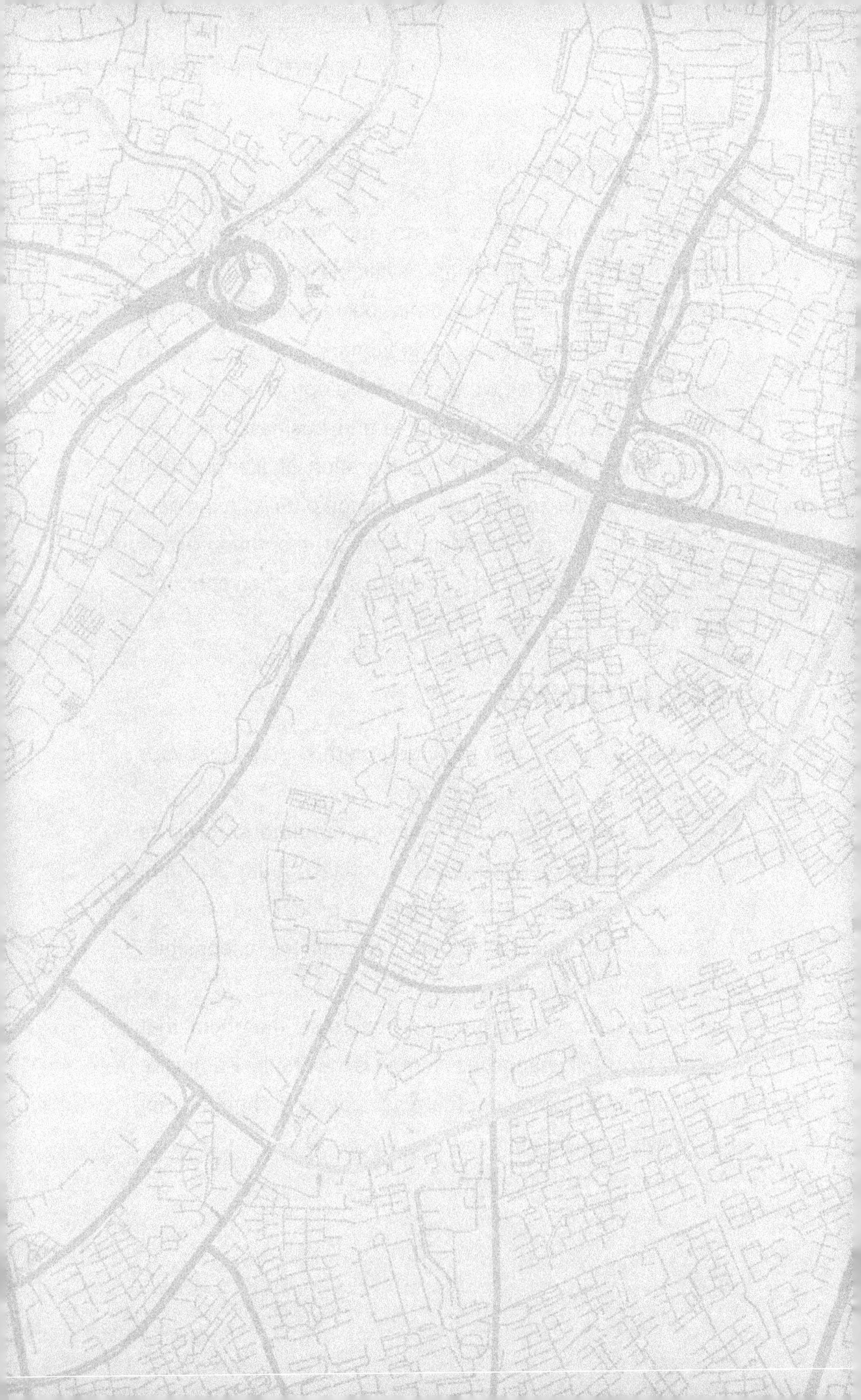

CHAPTER 7

INTEGRATION EXCELLENCE

———

In union, there is strength.[107]

–AESOP

In the previous chapter, we assessed the M&A process and its associated dynamics, which you will have to successfully navigate. In this chapter, we will address the integration process and how to best gain synergies and other benefits. Remember that integration exists solely to drive improvement.

First, we will identify where processes, systems, and talent upgrades are required. Subsequently, we will briefly discuss the team that will lead the execution of these integration efforts and the tools they will need to use. We will also determine what successful integration looks like. Finally, we will explore the concepts of culture, current state, and future state.

Before we dig deeper into the specifics around integration and growing your business, let us consider the following case study.

---

107 "Aesop Quotes," Goodreads, accessed November 10, 2025, https://www.goodreads.com/quotes/872676-in-union-there-is-strength.

CASE STUDY
PetSmart

In 1987, PetSmart (then Pet Food Warehouse) opened its first two shops.[108] After twenty-five years of sustained growth, the company obtained PE investment from BC Partners to take it to the next level.[109] This acquisition was valued at $8.7 billion.[110]

Through strategic expansion efforts, in 2017, the PE venture purchased Chewy—a pet care business—for $3.35 billion.[111] Several expansion-related challenges emerged as the management team attempted to integrate this new acquisition into the platform company (the company acquiring other companies). PetSmart was already facing operational inefficiency—and, some argue, poor management[112]—contributing to a 4.6 percent drop in same-store sales. The acquisition of Chewy further complicated matters with its massive financial leverage, financed largely through new debt. In addition, Chewy was an e-commerce giant, while PetSmart was dominant in the brick-and-mortar space. Reports indicate that the workforce subsequently

---

108 "Our Story," PetSmart Corporate, accessed August 28, 2025, https://www.petsmart-corporate.com/our-story/.

109 Ibid.

110 Ibid.

111 Jason Del Rey, "PetSmart Is Acquiring Chewy.com for $3.35 Billion in Largest E-Commerce Acquisition," CNBC, April 18, 2017, https://www.cnbc.com/2017/04/18/petsmart-buys-chewy.html.

112 Ryan Knutson and Jessica Mendoza, hosts, *The Journal*, "How PetSmart Solved Its Chewy Problem (featuring Miriam Gottfried)," WSJ Podcasts, December 3, 2019, https://www.wsj.com/podcasts/the-journal/how-petsmart-solved-its-chewy-problem/3cb86a84-133d-4a21-b19d-7981e90d1508.

faced a real culture shock from the substantial difference in corporate culture.[113] Additionally, in the early months following the sale, PetSmart suffered diminishing bond prices, indicating that investors were concerned that the acquisition was a bad investment.[114]

Fortunately, the company was able to address these integration challenges. By 2019, PetSmart took Chewy public, and by the end of the first day of public trading, Chewy was worth more than $13 billion. Since PetSmart had paid $3.3 billion to acquire the business, the $10 billion on-paper gain realized by BC Partners on the first day placed Chewy among the acquisitions with the most record-breaking returns that a PE firm had ever gotten.[115]

Some commentators attributed this phenomenal success to the ability of the business's leadership to recognize the immense value of Chewy before anyone else did.[116]

When confronted with opportunities for integration, are you able to see the genuine value that some smaller yet growing businesses possess? Is there room to sharpen your vision to see these opportunities clearly?

---

113 Dan Primack, "Behind PetSmart's $3.3 Billion Chewy Acquisition," Axios, April 19, 2017, https://www.axios.com/2017/12/15/behind-petsmarts-33-billion-chewy-acquisition-1513301711.

114 Knutson and Mendoza, "How PetSmart Solved Its Chewy Problem."

115 Ibid.

116 Ibid.

Identifying Deficiencies

Efficient and effective integration begins with identifying deficiencies. You must start by identifying where process, system, and talent upgrades are required.

PROCESSES

In process-related matters, you must determine whether the business has a lack of structure or inadequacies in its infrastructure. If you identify such deficiencies, you must build that infrastructure or structure to scale the business.

SYSTEMS

Systems encompass the technology infrastructure for data collection and sharing, such as phone systems, ERP systems, HR, accounting, and CRM. When you identify the systems the company has, you must assess if they are adequate. Where they are not, you must replace or plan to upgrade those systems. When you are managing complex or large organizations, the goal typically is to ensure the selection of systems is consistent and standard across all your business units. Examples of types of businesses that thrive with the incorporation of better systems are accounting and other financial services firms. Reports show that the top-performing firms in accounting can attribute their exceptional growth to M&A, better working conditions for staff, and efficiencies gained through systems such as automation or technology.[117]

To illustrate this point, here is a case study that highlights the importance of implementing better systems in PE ventures.

---

117   Courtney Vien, "The Astonishing Growth of PE-Backed CPA Firms," CFO Brew, October 18, 2024, https://www.cfobrew.com/stories/2024/10/18/ the-astonishing-growth-of-pe-backed-cpa-firms/.

CASE STUDY
Schellman Compliance

The numbers show that PE-backed accounting firms are overperforming and remain attractive to PE firms for future investment opportunities. One such company that validates this point of stellar performance is Schellman Compliance. Chris Schellman, a Florida-based accountant and entrepreneur, founded his auditing firm, Schellman Compliance, in the 2000s. In 2021, Lightyear Capital acquired majority shareholdership, at a time when Schellman was considering retirement.

With the inorganic growth from M&A, and with organic growth, the venture had purchased three firms in three years, with several deals still underway. Its organic growth was largely due to the establishment of a sales function—a development it did not have previously. In an article published by CFO Brew in 2024, the company's CFO, Avani Desai stated, "... to be sustainable in today's industry, you have to [have a dedicated sales function]. Referrals are great, and inbound is great, but we have to have an arm that does outbound."[118]

These are not the only system- and process-related improvements that Schellman made over the years to professionalize. A business intelligence system for KPIs is another system that the company implemented, leading to phenomenal success that the CFO referred to as "life-

---

118   Ibid.

changing."[119] The unstructured approach to decision-making was put aside in favor of data-driven execution, further increasing the efficacy of the business's systems. In reference to this, Desai said, "I was making decisions before kind of on gut and a little luck, and now we're still [using] a little gut and a little luck, but a lot of data."[120]

Through the availability of PE funds, the business was able to implement a comprehensive auditing software system that allowed the auditors full functionality to complete their business tasks that otherwise would have required multiple computer programs, including word processors and spreadsheet applications. Through this system, everyone's work is connected, and changes automatically update system-wide, with authorization to review these changes granted to the relevant managers.

As for the results of all these changes, Schellman was the 65th-largest IT auditing firm in the US in 2021, prior to making the PE deal, whereas after the deal, in 2024, it ranked 47th in the US. The firm's revenue mushroomed from $101.9 million to $148.5 million in 2023.[121]

The changes and advancements in systems made a tremendous difference to the growth and success of Schellman Compliance. An audit of your company's deficiencies regarding systems may uncover where your business can experience its biggest efficiency gains.

---

119 Ibid.

120 Ibid.

121 Ibid.

TALENT

Given the strategic analysis that informed your justification of a given acquisition, you must assert if you have the right management team in the right roles for the outcomes you intend on achieving with the business. This is like what the coach of a sports team does by assessing if the team has the athleticism needed for the game being played. Where you determine any gaps, you have options on how to remedy the disparities. You could organize training opportunities or other developmental activities for relevant staff. Whatever the case, such remedial activities must be contemplated and implemented.

Allocating a Team

Another aspect of integration is determining the team or individual to manage the overall integration process. A team tasked with managing integration may already exist in the PE firm or the company, or you may need to hire external advisors and/or consultants. The PE firm may elect operating partners who can serve in this capacity. You need dedicated and experienced professionals executing all the different integration work streams. You cannot leave it exclusively to the business that the platform company recently acquired.

Whoever the dedicated integration management team members are, they will be held accountable for the outcomes of the integration.

Selecting Tools

The platform operator is expected to already know what systems the acquired company will be equipped with. Though not always, the systems selected for the acquired company are typically the same as those employed by the platform operator itself. That is because it generally makes sense for the purpose of standardization and consistency across the company. The alternative, an unstandardized and inconsistent approach, is often more expensive and generally clumsy. By utilizing the same systems throughout, the company reaps cost-saving benefits and consistent operational processes and data flow. Therefore, if, for example, the platform operator uses one type of HR information system, they are likely to switch the smaller company to the same. This will likely aid in smoother and more effective communication, particularly for the generation of reports and other types of output. It is the same for all the other functions or aspects of the business, such as accounting, sales, operations, customer service, etc.

Your platform company and what you are already using are factors that influence the tools you choose as you seek synergies and opportunities to exercise financial prudence. You have your own calculus or working theory on why this tool is going to be the best choice. Once you have your genuine and reasonable justifications, you must select and install the actual tools that you have opted to use going forward. You must phase out disparate systems or tools across the board for ones that align better with the larger company in all areas.

Integration Projections and Success

You must have a clear vision as to what a successful integration process and outcome will look like. If you identify the necessary integration-related KPIs, they can assist you in measuring and monitoring the process. The KPIs relevant to your business will vary by deal structure and by PE firm. Therefore, it is incumbent upon you to determine the company's ideal integration KPIs. Also, consider that integration is time-bound and urgency is crucial. All relevant parties must be aware of the time-sensitivity around the implementation of the various work streams. For example, you cannot have a nine-month implementation of an activity that should only take three months. That would be a distraction and cause personnel stress, and it would subsequently negatively impact other connected activities. Therefore, the pressure of deadlines and the timely implementation of tasks must be impressed upon all responsible parties.

Regardless of how you measure progress, minimizing disruptions must be a priority. For example, if you are measuring customer cancellation rates or customer conversion rates, you must ensure that performance does not deteriorate during the integration. Ultimately, you are integrating for improvements, and any disruption is counterproductive. Therefore, you must be able to collect data and measure the initiatives that you are undertaking.

For example, once the integration is complete, are you experiencing expedited finalization of financial records? Is it now ten days, while it previously took twenty days? Are follow-ups more organized and efficient? Do you now have more data or better-quality data to make more informed decisions on the business activities, such as the speed with which the customer care department answers phone calls?

Ultimately, you want all those metrics to get better. As you undertake the process of changing out a system or even changing a process itself, you must ensure that the customer experience, the entity, and the organization continue to thrive.

Managing Culture

A vital yet often neglected component of integration is that of managing company culture. Perhaps—as it is not a system, a tool, or even a person—its intangible nature renders it forgettable or understated. Regardless, culture—both the current and future states—must be factored in. You may recall from chapter 2 (Accelerating Through Transformation), the pace in PE ventures is different than that in entrepreneurship. The disparity in pace may be a culture shock to the employees onboarding from the acquired business. This culture shock may affect their ability to adapt and perform in the business, subsequently culminating in the business struggling to meet its profitability goals.

Therefore, all staff must be made to understand the culture, particularly that the operating platform's culture is performance based. From observation, small businesses that have never operated in a performance-based culture find it challenging. All personnel must be taught and supported to understand how performance cultures run and the attitude or even social intelligence that is ideal for overall success.

On that note, helping personnel adapt to a shifting or new culture also requires social intelligence in the leadership team. "Shock therapy" or abrupt transitions do not work. However, an empathetic attitude toward the workforce struggling to adapt to the new culture does work.

If an acquired company had a laissez-faire company culture and a long-standing loyal and hardworking workforce, naturally, there may be friction. The business and its personnel will need support as they make the necessary adjustments to your faster, more structured, and high-accountability environment. In my experience, the adjustment challenges for small businesses from an entrepreneurial background are not only common but understandable. Thus, you must understand the current state of the company culture, determine your target state, and formulate a plan to achieve it. Educating the management team is more than a tactical effort; it is part of helping the workforce shift to the desired mindset. If this softer approach does not reap the necessary results, you may then need to employ an aggressive and decisive approach, including "shock therapy."

Developing the right culture requires an effective communication plan. You must repeat your message until it permeates through to everyone on your team. Otherwise, you risk the possibility of the business faltering due to employees not knowing what's transpiring or changing.

CASE STUDY
Jo-Ann Stores

Many experienced entrepreneurship ventures excel because they have a compelling or engaging company culture. If we cast our attention back to the earlier example of Joe & The Juice, you may recall how the company managed to retain its creative culture despite its impressive global expansion. Jo-Ann is another company with a creative culture that helped boost the business's growth. Jo-Ann Stores, a company offering fabric and craft products, was formed in 1943. Through continuous efforts, the company grew and was eventually acquired by Leonard Green & Partners for $1.6 billion.[122]

Then, friction ensued post-acquisition. The PE partners expected a data-driven approach, while the operators were used to a more creative one. Jo-Ann's culture was less hierarchical and more decentralized, while the PE partners expected centralization and standardization. Leonard

---

122 Megan Greenwell, "How Private Equity Killed the American Dream," *WIRED*, June 17, 2025, https://www.wired.com/story/megan-greenwell-bad-company-private-equity-interview/.

Green & Partners set their projections for 2011–2013 at a revenue growth of 8 percent initially, growing to 15 percent. The push for vibrant online growth and expansion inadvertently led to neglect of in-store quality and strained resources, exacerbated by the inefficiencies of insufficiently trained personnel.[123]

To address these challenges, the PE partners switched to a hybrid model and started workshops in the stores. With a budget of $20 million for training, they worked on integrating creativity and data skills. This, and town halls, increased employee satisfaction and reduced employee turnover by 10 percent in 2015.[124]

What concessions are you or your PE partners avoiding that you could make now? Are there any novel ways that you can approach integration and rectify any challenges that come along through an innovative approach?

CONCLUSION

In this chapter, we addressed the vital elements of successful integration, though our focus was primarily that of the platform company. In the next chapter, we will explore what you need to be aware of and what you need to do as you prepare to sell your business.

---

123 "10 Digital Transformation Challenges to Overcome," Univio, February 6, 2024, https://www.univio.com/blog/10-critical-digital-transformation-challenges-to-overcome/.

124 Barber and Goold, "The Strategic Secret of Private Equity."

KEY TAKEAWAYS

- Begin with the end in mind by deciding what a successful integration will look like, and work toward accomplishing that.
- Identify the key deficiencies, gaps, or even bottlenecks in your business—whether they are processes, systems, or talent related.
- Assemble a team and assign and/or hire an individual sufficiently competent to effectively manage the integration.
- Focus on consistency and standardization, particularly in the selection of tools and systems to optimize all-around performance and efficiency.
- Do not neglect the relevance of the present and future culture.
- Integration is a time-bound phase and must be conducted with urgency.
- Integration is for improvement.

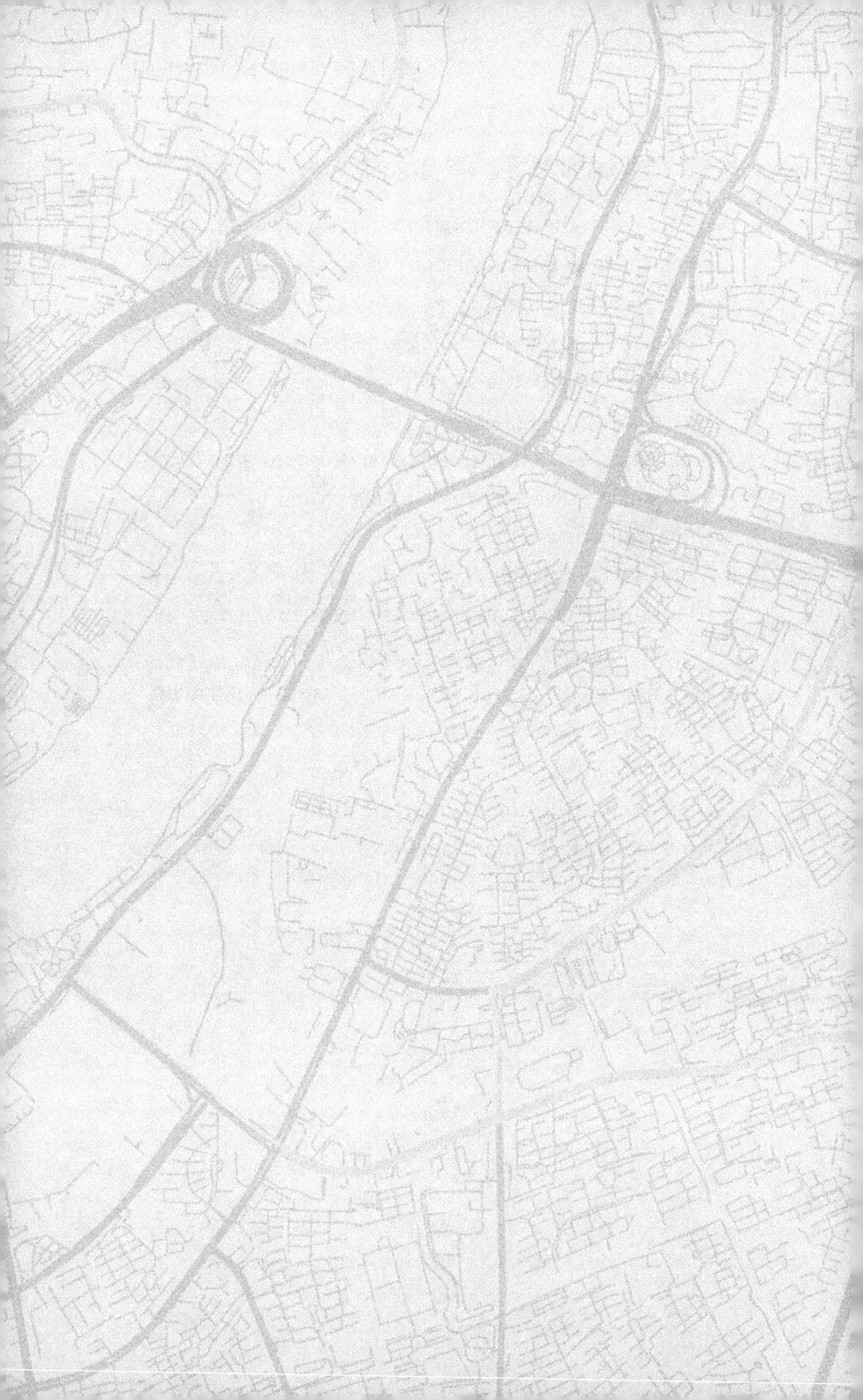

CHAPTER 8

PREPARING TO SELL

Have the end in mind and every day
make sure you're working toward it. [125]

—RYAN ALLIS, CO-FOUNDER OF ICONTACT

In chapter 7, we turned our attention to understanding how to excel at integration, the challenges it comes with, and how you can address those challenges. Now, we shall discuss a vital topic: preparation for the sale, which is the goal of PE. In this chapter, you will come to understand the PE firm's role in the selling process.

The PE firm typically decides on the right time to sell the company. In many cases, this happens without collaborating with the management team. There are various factors that impact the timing of the sale. These factors are both internal and external. The performance of the business, whether the PE firm is prioritizing fundraising at that time, and the period that the PE firm has held the investment (typically five years) are some of the most important internal factors.

---

125 "40 Inspiring Quotes About Business Growth — and Tips for Success,"
     Salesforce, September 19, 2025, https://www.salesforce.com/blog/
     inspirational-business-quotes/.

There is a plethora of elements you must consider from the external environment, including the timing for the market's receptivity to the sale of the company.

The Sales Process

As I have stated in other chapters, what you experience may be different from what I share with you here. However, here is the go-to-market process I have encountered time and time again.

You and the team put in the work for several years, and the PE firm finally believes it is time to sell. Once the PE firm makes the decision to go to market, based on the factors stated above, an investment bank is usually chosen to lead the sales process.

Thereafter, a "bake-off" happens. This is when the PE firm invites a select number of investment banks to pitch for the opportunity to be the business's partner in the sales process, brokering the deal. The PE firm is generally interested in working with an investment bank that is uniquely able to help realize outsized returns.

On your side of the table, your business is represented by a deal team, which you are likely part of. This deal team may include representatives from the PE firm, the actual partners of the firm, and whoever else represents management. Your team's mandate is to select the right sell-side investment bank for the business. Interviewing investment banks may require two days of consecutive meetings in a conference room with half a dozen or more representatives from the different banks. Each of these banks pitches to you why they are your best option to broker the sale of your company.

After each meeting, your team confers privately to discuss each investment bank you meet with. Collaboratively, you may use lists to assess each organization's virtues and what it has to offer. Together, you share the strengths and weaknesses you perceived from each option and eventually agree on which bank to work with.

Once you choose a bank to represent the business, you or other members of the management team need to spend time with the investment bank's representatives to intimately orient them to the performance of the business and other pertinent matters that may affect the sale. If the business was in the holding period for five years, for example, you must present them with all the financials, major or significant transitions, strategic decisions, and forecasts. Since the bank's representatives are going to present your business—potentially hundreds of times—to potential buyers, they must know how the business evolved on a granular level.

If the business experienced an abysmal financial year, a key decision-maker left the business, or you expanded the business into new territories, this information is important for your bankers to know. As such, it is your responsibility to provide them with this information so that they understand the story behind everything. You should anticipate questions as they acquire this information. If you have good investment banking partners, they will pressure test some of what you share with them. Their goal is to ensure you have a watertight business offer.

Once the investment bank has sufficient understanding of the business, it works with you to prepare the **business teaser**. The business teaser is a presentation or sales document that provides a potential buyer with information about the business's financials, management team, and relevant industry-level information. In it, you highlight the milestones the business aimed for along its journey and how those milestones were achieved. If we likened this sales process to that of selling a house, the business teaser is the equivalent of a listing for a house that is up for sale.

The business teaser presents the information in such a way that it creates excitement about the business's organic growth, number of acquisitions, successful integrations, great accomplishments, and future market opportunities. The bankers will send this teaser to potential buyers, and interested parties will respond by requesting further information. Thereafter, the bank may meet with these potential buyers over the phone or on communication platforms such as Zoom. During those conversations, interested parties will have the opportunity to ask whatever questions they have about the investment opportunity.

Throughout the process, which at this point is an auction, the bankers come back to the business's deal team with updates and information about their progress. They usually give those updates on a scheduled basis, typically weekly. You might want to use the opportunity to ask them various questions, such as:

- How's the auction process going?
- What's the market read on this?
- What are some of the questions you're fielding?
- What are some of the concerns you have heard?

At some point in this process, you must decide whether you have enough interested parties. If you estimate that you do, your bankers can send those parties requests for an **IOI**. As stated in chapter 6, an IOI is a document that shows one party's initial, yet nonbinding, interest in making a purchase in a business deal. The main goal is to assess the IOIs that are submitted and arrive at a more manageable and optimized short list of potential viable buyers.

This assessment of the offers includes analyzing the reputation of the firms interested in buying the company, the price they are willing to pay, and other factors that are utilized to determine the short list and ensure its quality. The reality is that you do not have the ability to deal with twenty or more people; the number must be manageable. Therefore, usually up to a half dozen firms end up becoming serious, short-listed potential buyers.

Based on this short list, your investment bankers, in collaboration with you or other members of the deal team, will schedule in-person management presentations. Depending on how many potential buyers are on your short list, you may need to arrange six to ten meetings. Each meeting is typically a half-day session, but it can be longer. During each session with the potential buyers, the management team walks through a detailed presentation called the **management presentation**, which can be a thirty- to forty-page slide deck.

During these sessions, the CEO, CFO, or whomever is tasked with the responsibility on that occasion answers any questions that the potential buyers have. You may note that there is no prescribed title that goes to this meeting; rather, the right people are responsible for participating in this discourse. The right people can include the founder, the CEO, the CFO, or a leader in operations. The CEO and CFO almost always attend, but various other members of the management team may attend as well. After those conversations take place, your bankers ask the potential buyers for their **LOIs.**

As you may recall from chapter 6, an LOI states the final offer to buy the company and all the conditions associated with it. Once the potential buyers submit their LOIs, the management team and the PE deal team decide on which buyer to transact with. This decision is largely based upon business valuation and, potentially, how the management presentations went. Assuming multiple firms submit similar purchase prices, to arrive at the optimal selection, you will need to consider answers to numerous questions, including these two basic yet important ones:

- Did the management team have a particular energy, impression, or culture that fit with that of the potential buyers that presented?

- Was there something about their industry knowledge or other businesses in the potential buyers' portfolios that made you believe they would be good stewards or partners moving forward?

Management Participation

Management will be responsible for pitching or presenting to potential buyers. As such, you must convey all the company's wonderful attributes and why it would make a great investment. The potential buyer could be any other entity, including another PE firm or a strategic buyer. A strategic buyer is a competitor in your space who is interested in purchasing your business. If your business is purchased by a strategic buyer, that buyer may not need or want you or members of your management team to continue to be involved in the business. Part of their calculus, maybe, is that your role is redundant. This is rarely personal, and in such cases, you must understand that you or your colleagues may not have jobs going forward and will need to chart new plans for yourselves.

PE firms typically hire investment banks to manage the sales process. Oftentimes, the PE firm already has relationships with investment banks and teams within those banks that it wants to work with, for various reasons. The reasons could include that the PE firm worked with them before in another business scenario, that the fee structure is attractive, or even that partners of the PE firm used to work at those banks. Regardless of the reasons for the selection of the investment bank, the complexities of the sale preparation are now between the management team and this investment bank.

Keep in mind that from the perspective of the management team, they may not have chosen or had the ability to participate in the process to choose the investment bank. This can become awkward and uncomfortable. The reason why there may be a level of friction is that management typically wants to engage with parties that understand the business and the industry. They want to work with people who have compatible personality types. They also want to make sure that this institution can get the best outcome. It is worth noting that this perspective or preference is not exclusive to management. The PE firm wants that too. But, as I mentioned before, there are various aspects to how they approach choosing bankers. Still, by involving the management team in the selection of the investment bank, the probability of selecting the best partner to broker the sale increases exponentially, in my opinion.

The Investment Bank

The investment bankers are brokers (intermediaries), not the actual buyers. Some brokers represent the buyer, and some represent the seller. These bankers, if they are buy-side bankers, have a collection of relationships that are useful for the sales process. The sell-side banker, therefore, represents you, the seller.

Here is a case in point.

> # CASE STUDY
> ## First Time
>
> Almost two decades ago, while serving as the CEO of a thriving business, I was informed that our PE partner was going to sell. As this was an outcome we had all been working toward, it came as no surprise. We had all worked hard and had generated exceptional results. So, naturally, I welcomed this decision. One thing that did surprise me, though, was that despite being the CEO, I was not invited by the PE firm to participate in the selection process of the investment bankers who would represent our company.
>
> I had thought it would have been reasonable to at least be given an audience to express my recommendation to select a different banker. My recommendation was not based on ego or the need for validation. On the contrary, I knew that the business needed an investment bank that truly knew the company well enough to represent it. In hindsight, I assume that the PE firm and the investment bank that it selected must have had a relationship that favored that selection. However, regardless of that, you still need brokers that understand the business. In the end, the company was not sold with that particular investment bank because it was unable to secure the most favorable outcomes. The PE firm utilized a different bank. This meant that the initial bank didn't get paid, because payment was based on the transaction from the deal.
>
> Since our business did not experience success with the first bank, the PE firm decided to take a different approach.

Partially because I had communicated to the PE partners my assessment of how to achieve a better outcome by involving the management team, they made sure to involve me and other members of the management team in the process of selecting our investment bank partner. On this occasion, the senior deal team partner of a PE firm asked me directly for input. This led to my intimate involvement in the selection process, or "bake-off," and being party to the decisions that ensued.

As it relates to the final selection of the banking partner, there is not a concrete approach to making the determination. It is sometimes based upon feel and perceived fit. Part of what helped us make well-thought-out decisions were the tools we devised for assessment purposes, such as simple pros-and-cons lists. These lists helped us critically assess our options and collaboratively make determinations.

In retrospect, if I had not been vocal about being excluded from the selection of the initial investment bank, it is possible the successful outcome we eventually had would have been different. When it becomes time to sell the business you are a part of, be sure to engage in the bank selection process. You will spend countless hours with the bankers, so it should be a group that you are comfortable with and that you believe can position your company for success.

Post-Sale Integration

Whatever the criteria, the PE team and the executive management team of the company decide who they're going to sell the business to. Thereafter, the potential buyer starts due diligence. This is the same due diligence process outlined in chapter 6 (The M&A Change), and post-close integration work will commence.

In some cases, there may not be much to integrate. It depends on who buys the company. If it's a PE firm that doesn't have any business like yours, it will likely treat the company as a platform, and there will be no integration. This is not to say that processes cannot be improved or that efficiencies will not be gained. There just won't be integration work until another company is purchased and added to this new platform.

In some cases, the buyer may be a strategic buyer, and it does not have to be a PE firm; it could be another firm in your industry. In that scenario, there is likely going to be integration work, and the firm may not need you or the other members of the executive management team. In fact, that may be part of the buyer's pre-purchase calculus and part of the economics around making this business deal work profitably. Accordingly, selling to a strategic buyer means accepting that you might have to transition to work elsewhere. This is a crucial possibility to keep in mind and is part of the reality of the PE venture.

If you are a founder and find yourself in this predicament, you obviously benefit financially. Naturally, how much you economically benefit from the sale depends upon your level of equity and the value created. Sometimes, founders and other executives genuinely just want to work, regardless of the economics. It is not uncommon to find that some have a passion for getting up in the morning and being part of a grand vision and being on a team or leading it. Money is not the key driver for everyone. We touched on the original founders of Tesla leaving the company in a previous case study. The case study that follows describes life after Tesla.

CASE STUDY
The Tesla Founders

While Elon Musk is one of the richest men in the world, the original founders, Martin Eberhard and Marc Tarpenning, remain juggernauts in the history of the evolution of transportation using clean energy. No doubt, the popularity of Tesla was birthed through their passion and vision. When Musk was handed the baton, he ran with the vision further than Eberhard and Tarpenning would have ever dreamed.

After Eberhard was ousted from Tesla, he worked for a venture capital firm, as he was not actively in search of new work opportunities in the automotive industry. Thereafter, he was approached by Volkswagen to join its electric vehicle program, and he took the company up on the offer. His presence there was short-lived, as his approach clashed with some of the top-leadership strategies that promoted solutions such as "smart diesel." Eberhard found that contradictory to the concept of clean energy, which he championed. His efforts at the time were focused on faster adoption of electric vehicles.

At present, Eberhard regards himself as retired and appears to be living a slower yet full life with his wife on an undisclosed island. Eberhard, in late 2025, still owned some Tesla stocks and remained very financially secure, stating that "… there is such a thing as enough money" and adding that "his kids will be fine, and he lives in a beautiful home without aspiring to be a 'jillionaire.'"[126]

Marc Tarpenning co-founded not only Tesla with Eberhard but also their previous business, called NuvoMedia. This was the company that produced the Rocket eBook—the first e-reader, before Kindle even existed. Tarpenning left Tesla at the time the company was engineering the Model S sedan. Back in 2019, he stated that he sometimes speaks to Musk. Furthermore, Tarpenning stated that he had no regrets, adding, "The whole thing was wonderful from the beginning to the end. It was, you know, the worst and the best. And it's worked out great."[127]

Both Tarpenning[128] and Eberhard[129] still invest in various startup projects.

If you intend to transition to new work opportunities, given your experience, can you see that you have more options than you may first have considered?

---

126   Kim Java, host, "Tesla's Forgotten Founder Speaks Out – Exclusive w/ Martin Eberhard," August 28, 2024, YouTube, https://www.youtube.com/watch?v=88KHfX_kPIY.

127   Martin Eberhard and Marc Tarpenning, "Tesla Founders Martin Eberhard and Marc Tarpenning Talk About the Early Days and Bringing on Elon Musk," interview by Lora Kolodny, CNBC, February 6, 2021, https://www.cnbc.com/2021/02/06/tesla-founders-martin-eberhard-marc-tarpenning-on-elon-musk.html.

128   Adam Hayes, "Tesla: The True Untold Story," Investopedia, updated September 8, 2025, https://www.investopedia.com/articles/personal-finance/061915/story-behind-teslas-success.asp.

129   "Martin Eberhard – Investor Timeline," Crunchbase, accessed October 31, 2025, https://www.crunchbase.com/person/martin-eberhard/person_overview_investor/timeline.

CONCLUSION

In this chapter, we addressed the sales process that you, and the rest of the team, have spent several years working toward. The steps outlined in this chapter, if adhered to, can help increase the possibility of a great outcome for you.

KEY TAKEAWAYS

Here are some of the key points you need to keep in mind:

- To increase the business's odds of selecting the best investment bank, the PE firm should include the management team in the selection process.
- The buyer may choose to retain you as part of the management team, in the same role, or offer you another position. They may also feel that you are not a good fit for the business going forward or that your role is redundant. You must be aware of these possibilities and prepare yourself accordingly.

CHAPTER 9

WHAT'S NEXT?

___

*You must always be able to predict what's next
and then have the flexibility to evolve.*[130]

—MARC BENIOFF, CEO AND FOUNDER OF SALESFORCE

In the previous chapter, we discussed how to effectively prepare for the sale of your business. In this final chapter, we turn our attention to you and your future. Have you given enough thought to what will happen to you after the sale? After years of fixing the business, buying complementary businesses, and creating value in several ways, you will sell. That is what you have been working hard toward. If your intention is a career in PE, then you will have to do it all over again, many times.

Naturally, with an exit comes change. The reality of the business getting a new owner means you should prepare yourself specifically for this ownership change. Some of the mental and emotional prepa-

---

130   Salesforce, "40 Inspiring Quotes About Business Growth."

rations that you need to make are to understand that you may not have clarity about the outcome for a while and that, even if you have clarity about what will happen to the business, knowing the outcome still requires you to prepare yourself for any transition that results. That includes the possibility that you may eventually have to change your role.

When we look at previous eras, in particular the era of blue-chip companies, employees tended to work for the same company for decades—in some cases, their entire career. In our time, particularly in the case of PE businesses, the situation is entirely different. For portfolio company leadership teams, the reality is not for the meek: If the business is sold, you must be comfortable with the unknown. That requires a level of confidence in yourself and your abilities. From my observation, the type of people who flourish in this environment throughout their careers are those who feel excited about new possibilities and a new challenge every four or five years. If you are an individual who enjoys continuous learning, innovating, and building something through various stages, I am confident you will thrive in a lifelong PE career. However, if you are attracted to a type of career path that is static and somewhat predictable, PE may not be your long-term destination. Therefore, let us discuss each of the options you may have after the sale. These options include staying with the business (with its new owner), leaving and pursuing other options, or opportunities with the current PE firm.

Stay with the Business

If the business is sold to a company that does not have a similar operation, the new owner often wants to retain the management team. In many cases, that is the most appealing part of the deal because of the executive management team's demonstrated success. When buying a new platform company, there is usually an expectation that the management team and the CEO go with it.

At the time of exit, the management team typically owns 20 percent of the equity. The new buyer will likely want to ensure their interests are aligned. Subsequently, they may request that the members of the executive management team put a certain percentage of equity back into the company. This type of equity is referred to as **rolling equity** or **rollover equity**, which means "… either retaining partial ownership in your practice or investing a portion of your sale proceeds into the purchasing organization. For example, if your practice sells for $5 million, you might choose to roll 30 percent of that value into continued ownership."[131] Rolling equity adds more reasons for the management team to remain committed because they still have direct financial interests tied to the business's success or failure.

If you intend to stay in the business, it is important you understand the strategy of the new owners and how they plan to grow the company over the next few years. Staying may mean one of two options:

- **In the same role**: This means you retain your title and role, without any changes. In this instance, you may be expected to invest.

- **In the same business but a different role**: The new owners may value your contribution but require you to serve in a different role. For example, if you are the CEO of a $100 million business that's acquired by a billion-dollar platform company, the new owners may state that they already have a

---

131   "What Is Rolling Equity? Definition and Tips for Successful Negotiations," Practice Transitions Group, accessed October 30, 2025, https://practicetransitionsgroup. com/blog/what-is-rolling-equity-definition-and-tips-for-successful-negotiations/.

CEO in the holding company. Therefore, they may offer you a leadership role in a division of the business. That means you still run part of the new company but now report to a boss who oversees the entire organization. In this case, you need to decide if this new reporting structure is for you. The changes will no doubt impact your gravitas, and you will be a small part of a much bigger operation.

- **Leave and pursue other options.**

For whatever reason, the buying company may make the determination that it no longer needs your and the management team's services. Alternatively, you and/or your team members may decide that you don't want to partner with the new ownership group. Either way, you will need to consider what is next, and the sooner the determination is made the better.

CASE STUDY
Self-Exiting

During my career in PE, I have had to let dozens of people go because they proved not to be the best fit for the future of the companies. On one occasion, a business I was running was sold to a new buyer. During diligence, it became clear that the CFO did not have the capabilities that the buyers felt they needed for the business. It is worth noting that this individual was good in the role he originally held but, unfortunately, lacked the necessary acumen for the role's new responsibilities under new ownership, especially regarding the expected growth.

So, the buyers approached me two or three months before the deal closed and asked me to consider a change of CFO. During the discussion, they shared their rationale, and I assessed it objectively and found it to be reasonable. Therefore, I agreed to make the necessary adjustment.

At the conclusion of our last management presentation, I informed the CFO that he would not be a part of the business post-sale. Naturally, he was disappointed; I would have been, too, if the tables were turned. At that point, he had already conveyed excitement about joining the new PE business. He had been willing to attempt to step up to the challenge. However, when I brought up this decision, I also pointed out the deficiencies that the buyers had noted and that I had agreed with. With understandable reserve, he assessed the argument and agreed. With objectivity, he realized that the company was looking for someone with other capabilities for the next phase of its evolution.

As stated in previous chapters, I like to extend support to members of the team who have proven themselves to be assets, even when it is time for them to leave. In this case, I helped find this CFO a new job by making some calls and acting as one of his references. Eventually, he found a good job elsewhere. Truth be told, had he stayed, he probably would have failed. Some might ask, why didn't you just train him to "future-proof" him for the responsibilities of his role once it evolved? Though he could have been trained, the nature of PE does not typically allow the time necessary to train someone into the position. These types of businesses are usually looking for someone who can hit the ground running, so to speak.

In addition, this was not a talent or skills challenge that six months of training would have addressed. He simply didn't have the experience or capabilities, and the PE firm was already aware of this before the deal was consummated.

Similarly, you, or another member of the management team, may assess that you are not a good fit for the new business. In such circumstances, out of courtesy, the management team may communicate that they will inform the PE firm of their decision to opt out in advance. It is vital that this is conveyed in good time in case their ongoing service was a factor that the buyers weighed for the transaction. Having been in this situation myself, here is one of my experiences.

CASE STUDY
Choosing to Leave

After I led a successful business as its president, the PE firm was ready to exit. The business was the leader in a particular product category, and a strategic buyer snapped it up. This strategic buyer happened to be a competitor who had struggled to enter the market that we had skillfully developed up to that point. Among what we excelled at were a global manufacturing and distribution pipeline and an excellent sales force. This strategic buyer realized that the smarter move was not to compete with our business but to buy it instead. So, they did, and our company was folded into this former competitor's operation.

The exit was successful, and so were the outcomes. The management reaped healthy returns, and so did the business. The new owners approached me and asked if I would be willing to run another part of their company. In this new arrangement, I served in a greater role and had more overall responsibility. However, there was one major problem that I had not fully anticipated: The platform company was an eighty-year-old family business. At that time, the chairman of that company was third generation and had already announced the elderly owner's son-in-law as the next chairman.

Coming from a fast-paced working environment, I realized that this new culture was starkly different. It was slow; it ran at a pace that felt alien to me. What's more, one could easily argue that the most significant challenge of the business was that it was nepotistic. With my background in PE—and particularly companies such as GE Capital, where meritocracy is the order of corporate governance—I found this less than ideal.

After making a careful assessment of the dynamics at this family-owned enterprise, it was clear to me that I had to leave. This turned out to be a great decision, as I soon found a role that aligned with my desire for a brisker pace and rewarding team members based on merit.

If the buying company decides not to bring you along (e.g., after you served the business for the past twenty years), it may offer you a severance or separation agreement. Within that agreement regarding some sort of compensation, they may ask you not to compete with certain businesses for a specified period. It is not uncommon for a company to offer up to a year's salary if the outgoing member of the team commits to not competing with the business for one year or longer. Therefore, you would need to figure out what your alternatives for gainful employment would be for that time if you were to sign the noncompete agreement. This may be a challenge if all your experience is in one field or industry.

There have been many legislative developments and court cases pertaining to the enforcement of noncompete agreements. Some wonder if those agreements are truly legally enforceable. The company may contend that it may be difficult for or financially detrimental to the firm if you decline signing a noncompete agreement. However, if you are leaving the business on good terms, it may be possible to work with the business on a structure that provides you with gainful employment opportunities without harming your former employer.

Consider the following case study pertaining to the enforceability of noncompete agreements.

CASE STUDY
Noncompete Clauses and Clashes

The global discourse around noncompete clauses appears to be heating up. Here are several examples, beginning with the widespread ban in the US that the previous administration wanted to enforce.

In September 2025, the US government stopped fighting the ban on all noncompete agreements that the previous administration's Federal Trade Commission wanted to enforce back in 2024. Though judges had blocked the broad ban, the Biden administration wanted to appeal. Under the Trump administration, the government decided to let the appeal die; therefore, the widespread ban is dead, and state-wide laws apply.[132]

In one UK case that concluded in 2018, a plumber opted to change employment and was informed by his previous employer that he could not work in a rival capacity for up to one year. He found this unacceptable and took the business to court. The court eventually ruled that the business's stipulation was excessive and would only be acceptable if it was for a more reasonable period and if it truly protected the business's secrets.[133]

Lim Teck Yong, a former high-level executive of Shopee, faced challenges changing jobs when Shopee sought a court order to stop him from attaining a new role at its competitor, TikTok. In a 2024 judgment, the court ruled that the company's rule lacked sufficient merit because the noncompete clause was too broad. As Yong had already commenced employment at TikTok, the court allowed him to continue at his new place of work.[134]

Meanwhile, in South Africa in 2024, a car dealership (24 Motors) succeeded in blocking the future employment opportunities with competitors for several of their former

---

132 Daniel Wiessner, "Trump Administration Drops Defense of Ban on Employee 'Non-compete' Agreements," Reuters, September 5, 2025, https://www.reuters.com/legal/litigation/trump-administration-drops-defense-ban-employee-noncompete-agreements-2025-09-06/.

133 Pimlico Plumbers Ltd. v. Smith (2018) UKSC 29, https://supremecourt.uk/uploads/uksc_2017_0053_press_summary_fc5d49d452.pdf.

134 Shopee Singapore Pte. Ltd. v. Lim Teck Yong (2024) SGHC 29, https://www.elitigation.sg/gd/gd/2024_SGHC_29/pdf.

employees. This was for up to twelve months.[135] Another case in South Africa took place in the previous year—a prominent case called the Sadan case. In this case, two former employees were sued by Workforce Staffing (Pty) Ltd. The company wanted to bar these former employees, Tazneem Sadan and Nicholas Arajuo, from working for competitors. Sadan and Arajuo had already started working for the competition after leaving, but Workforce Staffing wanted the courts to ensure they could not do so for up to two years. The courts ultimately ruled that the two-year timeframe was too long and changed it to one year to extend fairer rights to the former employees.[136]

If you decide to leave your current employment, it would be wise to become well-versed in what a noncomplete agreement would mean for you if your employer requires you to sign one.

Potential Opportunity with the Exiting PE Firm

Staying or leaving to work at a similar business are not your only options. Another option that may be open to you is working for the PE firm that has just exited the business. Assuming there has been a successful exit, and your business has been sold to a company that you don't wish to work for—or at which there is no role for you, in some instances—the PE firm may ask you to work at or for their firm.

Also, if you have developed a good reputation, other PE firms may reach out to you to see if you can assist their ventures. This is not

---

135   Twenty Four Motors CC t/a Ford Ermelo v. Andries Johannes Jacobus Venter and Others (2024) ZALCJHB 33, https://www.saflii.org/za/cases/ZALCJHB/2024/33.pdf.

136   Sadan and Another v. Workforce Staffing (Pty) Ltd. (2023) ZALAC 14, http://www.saflii.org/za/cases/ZALAC/2023/14.html.

an uncommon outcome, as PE firms want to work with people with whom they have had successful working relationships in the past or who have a track record of success at other PE-backed ventures. This is largely because it can be hard to find the right talent or good partners. Therefore, they may wish to work with those they have worked with before on different tours of duty.

Retire or Semiretire

After considering all the different options addressed above, you may consider yourself at a place and age where you don't want or need to work at all—or, if you do, you can be choosy. In this instance, you might decide that this was your last full-time job. This could mean focusing on pursuing more of your passions, family-related activities, and lifestyle events while still working infrequently. Whether retired or semiretired, you can decide to participate on boards or do nonprofit work to stay mentally stimulated and retain life satisfaction in your golden years.

CASE STUDY
Golfing Partner

On one Saturday afternoon, I was out playing golf with a retired friend of mine. He had completed a successful decades-long career in PE that culminated in him retiring several years prior. As we walked on the lush grass of the sprawling golf course, he shared with me what was keeping him busy at the age of seventy. My golfing companion sat on three public boards and one PE board. These commitments led to him travelling all over the country and engaging with the management of each organization. Sometimes, this meant meeting with these executives and quizzing them in the office. Other times, it was a more relaxed conversation over dinner. All of it was real work.

When my friend shared with me how busy his day-to-day schedule was, I was surprised. Didn't he devote decades of his working life to eventually have this time to rest? I could not wrap my head around why anyone would stay so busy after retirement. So, I asked him, and he explained, "Ty, it's not about the money anymore."

At some point, my friend had realized that the key to ongoing good health, well-being, and longevity was staying active. Fortunately, the man was driven and a type A personality. He shared that if a person is healthy, has energy, and is wired the way he was, they just don't stop.

My friend said, as he reflected on the outcome for many of his fellow retirees who entered their senior years without activities to keep them stimulated and invigorated, "If they stop, they die."

I understood my friend to mean that he still had a compelling sense of purpose. Staying active was a natural by-product of living out that purpose. Research (specifically in the US) backs up this premise: People who retire early increase their probability of dying early.[137] This is particularly true for men compared with women. To be clear, I am not advocating for executives to keep working when they are far

---

137 Maria D. Fitzpatrick and Timothy J. Moore, "The Mortality Effects of Retirement: Evidence from Social Security Eligibility at Age 62," *Journal of Public Economics* 157 (January 2018): 121–37, https://doi.org/10.1016/j.jpubeco.2017.12.001.

beyond exhausted. Rather, I am saying that whatever you do, always retain a sense of purpose that adds to your life's meaning.

CONCLUSION

In this chapter, we discussed your options after a sale and some possibilities that you can explore to ensure a seamless and positive transition. The PE firm controls the destiny of the business and is responsible for the ultimate decision of who will buy the business, based on the best economic output, by and large. This means you have little or no control over what options will be open to you when the time comes to exit.

KEY TAKEAWAYS

- There must be an exit.
- You must prepare yourself for whatever eventuality comes your way so that you are not blindsided and negatively impacted.

Conclusion

I reminded myself that a beginning and an ending are
two different places, and, in real life,
you might be able to make your own ending,
whatever had gone before.[138]

—STEPHANIE BUTLAND IN *LOST FOR WORDS*

After investing time to read through all nine chapters, we are now finally at the conclusion. Hopefully, you have come to a deeper understanding of everything you need to know beyond the deal.

In **chapter one**, we uncovered the key mindset shifts you need to make for PE success. If you take anything away from this book, at the very least know that you will have to shift your mindset because when you enter PE, the relationship dynamic is different, and there are very different accountability dynamics than those you may be used to.

In **chapter two**, we explored the pace of change and what you need to understand about navigating the transformation. We learned about the PE timeline, how to prioritize, and the necessity of re-strategizing if the situation calls for such adjustments.

---

138 "Beginnings and Endings Quotes," Goodreads, accessed October 25, 2025, https://www.goodreads.com/quotes/tag/beginnings-and-endings/.

The language of PE is completely different and requires an investment of time and effort to learn. Regardless of how you learn the terminology and overall language—whether through courses, mentorship, or other means—you must acquire these skills to be a successful operator. Operating with PE financial literacy as your foundational understanding not only helps you speak the same language as your PE partners but also allows you to work together in alignment. This was discussed in **chapter three**.

In **chapter four**, we considered the necessity of making upgrades where the business's leadership sees fit. This process requires a clear-eyed and unemotional perspective. This is particularly true when it comes to your team's capabilities and their ability to meet the expectation of the PE firm to deliver on financial commitments. Achieving this clarity and objectivity involves being honest with yourself and making the changes that are necessary as soon as you can to make sure you have the best talent you can find and afford.

Advocating with the board is the topic we turned to in **chapter five**. In this chapter, we learned how best to leverage the relationships with, and the skill sets of board members while at the same time developing relationships that are useful and productive, with the understanding that you are likely going to be interacting with these individuals often and for several years. Knowing that you are meeting them frequently, not just every quarter, effective advocacy with the board involves deciding how you can effectively gain and leverage their support and create a rhythm with them.

It is worth emphasizing that board members are not your friends, nor are they your adversaries. They are your business partners. Therefore, you must develop the skill to work with them both as individuals and as members of a group, because the dynamic is different in group settings.

In **chapter six**, we focused on the changes you need to manage in the M&A phases. M&A is a viable and popular growth strategy that your company may wish to employ. Exceptional time management is required to navigate the M&A dynamics. This is due to the strain on finite resources (such as time) that this requires, in addition to whatever other daily business responsibilities you already have. As you navigate the M&A dynamics, be honest. Never promise your staff that nothing will change because change is inevitable. Rather, be committed to helping them navigate any changes that may come along.

To any high-performing business, excellence is important. In **chapter seven**, we turned our attention to excellence in integration. This is a vital exercise. Do not underestimate the importance of successfully integrating acquisitions. Without successful integration, the acquisition itself may end up being worthless.

Preparing to sell was the subject of **chapter eight**. Here, we emphasized that the CEO and management team should try to be involved in the investment bank selection process. This is sometimes overlooked, but it is highly important. Selling the business is a time-intensive and often complicated process. The CEO and the management team will have to continue to drive the performance of the business while going through the sales process. The business must continue to perform well during this process. The sales process is an added burden for the management team that must still be undertaken. You must understand how to be involved and how to develop a story around the future of the business. Selecting the right bankers will play a pivotal part in realizing successful outcomes of the sales process.

Finally, in **chapter nine**, we considered the main options open to you after the sale. There are different options, depending upon your situation. Before a sale takes place, you must determine what the role of the leader and the leadership team is going to be moving forward.

Be transparent about expectations. At the same time, be prepared for the fact that you or your team may not be part of the new business or part of the purchase by the acquirer. As we saw in this chapter, if that is the case, you still have options open to you that you can consider and that may be equally or even more fulfilling. If you can understand and even prepare for every eventuality, you can compartmentalize during this process. Compartmentalizing may increase the probability that you will enjoy a more optimized and stable emotional and mental state, regardless of what comes next for you. This preparation is, in essence, an exercise for the greater good, even if the outcome is not what you wanted.

In closing, I hope this book met your expectations and that you acquired knowledge that will save you time, effort, and even frustration. The PE journey is often exciting and sometimes nerve-wracking. With the knowledge I shared in the pages of this book, going forward, I hope your journey features more of the former and less of the latter.

With gratitude, I wish you success on your PE journey as you traverse the path beyond the deal.

References

1.   Coffey, Adam. *The Wise Exit*. "How to Win with Private Equity with Adam Coffey." Hosted by Brian D. Califano, October 10, 2023. Spotify, 12:51. https://open.spotify.com/episode/2coJBF6vOM8Du9PyJKKF9D.

2.   Chen, James. "Private Equity." Investopedia, May 16, 2025. Accessed November 10, 2025. https://www.investopedia.com/terms/p/privateequity.asp.

3.   Drucker, Peter F. *The Effective Executive*. Butterworth-Heinemann, 1999.

4.   Fairway Market. "About Fairway." Fairway Market. Accessed July 16, 2025. https://www.fairwaymarket.com/about-fairway/.

5.   Dan Glickberg Food. *Dan Glickberg Food*. Accessed July 16, 2025. https://www.danglickbergfood.com/.

6.   Reddy, Sumathi. "Fairway Grocery Chain Targets an Expansion." *The Wall Street Journal*, July 11, 2011. https://www.wsj.com/articles/SB100014240527023047606004576427983426433672.

7.   Reddy, Sumathi. "Fairway Grocery Chain Targets an Expansion." *The Wall Street Journal*, July 11, 2011. https://www.wsj.com/articles/SB10001424052702304760604576427983426433672.

8.   Wasserman, Noam. *The Founder's Dilemmas: Anticipating and Avoiding the Pitfalls That Can Sink a Startup*. Princeton University Press, 2012.

9.   Barber, Felix, and Goold, Michael. "The Strategic Secret of Private Equity." *Harvard Business Review* 85, no. 9 (2007): 53–61.

10.   Zeisberger, C., Prahl, M., and White, B. *Private Equity in Action: Case Studies from Developed and Emerging Markets*. Wiley, 2017.

11.   *Crain's New York Business*. "Fairway Struggles in Public Spotlight." March 17, 2014. https://www.crainsnewyork.com/article/20140317/HOSPITALITY_TOURISM/303169982/fairway-struggles-in-public-spotlight.

12.   Appelbaum, Eileen, and Park, Andrew W. "How Private Equity Ruined a Beloved Grocery Chain." *The Atlantic*, February 16, 2020. https://www.theatlantic.com/ideas/archive/2020/02/how-private-equity-ruined-fairway/606625/.

13.   Batt, R. and Appelbaum, E. "Private Equity Pillage: Grocery Stores and Workers at Risk." *The American Prospect*, October 26, 2018. https://prospect.org/power/private-equity-pillage-grocery-stores-workers-risk/.

14.   Bloomberg. "Fairway Returns to Bankruptcy, Aims to Sell Manhattan Stores." *Bloomberg*, January 22, 2020. https://www.bloomberg.com/news/articles/2020-01-22/fairway-said-

to-seek-bankruptcy-that-keeps-some-stores-open?embedded-checkout=true.

15. Goleman, Daniel. *Emotional Intelligence: Why It Can Matter More Than IQ.* Bantam Books, 1997.

16. Encyclopedia.com. "Orfalea, Paul." *Encyclopedia of Economics and Business.* Last modified 2020. Accessed November 3, 2025. https://www.encyclopedia.com/education/economics-magazines/orfalea-paul.

17. Encyclopedia.com. "Orfalea, Paul." *Encyclopedia of Economics and Business.* Last modified 2020. Accessed November 3, 2025. https://www.encyclopedia.com/education/economics-magazines/orfalea-paul.

18. Encyclopedia.com. "Orfalea, Paul." *Encyclopedia of Economics and Business.* Last modified 2020. Accessed November 3, 2025. https://www.encyclopedia.com/education/economics-magazines/orfalea-paul.

19. Schawbel, Dan. "Paul Orfalea on Creating the Kinko's Brand." *Forbes*, June 28, 2012. https://www.forbes.com/sites/danschawbel/2012/06/28/paul-orfalea-on-creating-the-kinkos-brand/.

20. Dan Schawbel, "Paul Orfalea on Creating the Kinko's Brand." *Forbes*, June 28, 2012. https://www.forbes.com/sites/danschawbel/2012/06/28/paul-orfalea-on-creating-the-kinkos-brand/.

21. O'Shaughnessy, Patrick. *Invest Like the Best.* Episode 299, "Paul Orfalea - It's About the Money." Spotify, October 18, 2022. https://open.spotify.com/episode/3x3xmrYHaFlUJsik4lx0IJ.

22.   O'Shaughnessy, Patrick. *Invest Like the Best*. Episode 299, "Paul Orfalea - It's About the Money." Spotify, October 18, 2022. 00:49:00. https://open.spotify.com/episode/3x3xmrYHaFlUJsik4lx0IJ.

23.   Corporate Finance Institute. "Entry Multiple." Accessed July 19, 2025. https://corporatefinanceinstitute.com/resources/valuation/entry-multiple/.

24.   "100+ Entrepreneur Quotes." American Express. May 4, 2024. Accessed September 25, 2025. https://www.americanexpress.com/en-us/business/blueprint/resource-center/start/100-quotes-from-successful-entrepreneurs.

25.   PitchBook. "Company Profile: Valuation, Investors, Acquisition." Accessed August 17, 2025. https://pitchbook.com/profiles/company/58377-52#overview.

26.   Innovosales. "[CASE STUDY] How a Private Equity Portfolio Company Created a Turnaround Success." Innovosales, February 15, 2022. https://innovosales.com/blog/case-study-how-a-private-equity-portfolio-company-created-a-turnaround-success/.

27.   PE Hub. "Audax-Backed Smart Care Buys Horizon Bradco." PE Hub, August 30, 2021. https://www.pehub.com/audax-backed-smart-care-buys-horizon-bradco/.

28.   Innovosales. "[CASE STUDY] How a Private Equity Portfolio Company Created a Turnaround Success." Innovosales, February 15, 2022. https://innovosales.com/blog/case-study-how-a-private-equity-portfolio-company-created-a-turnaround-success/.

29. Innovosales. "[CASE STUDY] How a Private Equity Portfolio Company Created a Turnaround Success." Innovosales, February 15, 2022. https://innovosales.com/blog/case-study-how-a-private-equity-portfolio-company-created-a-turnaround-success/.

30. Innovosales. "[CASE STUDY] How a Private Equity Portfolio Company Created a Turnaround Success." Innovosales, February 15, 2022. https://innovosales.com/blog/case-study-how-a-private-equity-portfolio-company-created-a-turnaround-success/.

31. Innovosales. "[CASE STUDY] How a Private Equity Portfolio Company Created a Turnaround Success." Innovosales, February 15, 2022. https://innovosales.com/blog/case-study-how-a-private-equity-portfolio-company-created-a-turnaround-success/.

32. Innovosales. "[CASE STUDY] How a Private Equity Portfolio Company Created a Turnaround Success." Innovosales, February 15, 2022. https://innovosales.com/blog/case-study-how-a-private-equity-portfolio-company-created-a-turnaround-success/.

33. Joe & The Juice. "JOE History." Joe & The Juice. Accessed August 18, 2025. https://www.joejuice.com/culture/joe-history.

34. Bloomberg. "General Atlantic Agrees to Buy Majority Stake in Joe & the Juice." *Bloomberg*, November 13, 2023. https://www.bloomberg.com/news/articles/2023-11-13/general-atlantic-agrees-to-buy-majority-stake-in-joe-the-juice.

35. Valedo Partners. "Joe & The Juice." Valedo Partners. Accessed August 18, 2025. https://www.valedopartners.com/en/joe-the-juice/.

36. "DKK to USD - Danish Krone to US Dollar Conversion." Exchange-Rates.org. Last modified August 18, 2025. Accessed November 10, 2025. https://www.exchange-rates.org.

37. Valedo Partners. "Joe & The Juice." Valedo Partners. Accessed August 18, 2025. https://www.valedopartners.com/en/joe-the-juice/.

38. Rouen, Ethan, and Suraj Srinivasan. "Joe & The Juice Crosses the Atlantic." Harvard Business School Multimedia/Video Case 118-039, November 2017. https://www.hbs.edu/faculty/Pages/item.aspx?num=53585.

39. Les Deux. "A Curious Case in Culture - Kaspar Basse, Founder of Joe & The Juice." Accessed August 18, 2025. https://lesdeux.com/blogs/explore/kaspar-basse-founder-of-joe-and-the-juice-a-curious-case-in-culture.

40. Les Deux. "A Curious Case in Culture - Kaspar Basse, Founder of Joe & The Juice." Accessed August 18, 2025. https://lesdeux.com/blogs/explore/kaspar-basse-founder-of-joe-and-the-juice-a-curious-case-in-culture.

41. Raphael, Rina. "Coffee, Sandwich, and a Side of Edgy: How Joe & The Juice Aims to Take Over the U.S." *Fast Company*, January 11, 2017. https://www.fastcompany.com/3066489/coffee-sandwich-and-a-side-of-edgy-how-joe-the-juice-aims-to-take-over-the.

42. Morse, Gardiner. "Trust, but Verify." *Harvard Business Review*, May 2005. https://hbr.org/2005/05/trust-but-verify.

43. "Toys 'R' Us, Inc. History." *International Directory of Company Histories*, Vol. 57. St. James Press, 2004. Accessed November 5, 2025. https://www.fundinguniverse.com/company-histories/toys-r-us-inc-history/.

44. Ryan, Tom. "Should Toys "R" Us Be Toying With Flagships Again?" RetailWire, October 5, 2023. https://retailwire.com/discussion/should-toysrus-be-toying-with-flagships-again/.

45. Misamore, Brian. "Breaking Down the Demise of Toys "R" Us." *Harvard Business School Online*, April 10, 2018. https://online.hbs.edu/blog/post/breaking-down-the-demise-of-toys-r-us.

46. Misamore, Brian. "Breaking Down the Demise of Toys "R" Us." *Harvard Business School Online*, April 10, 2018. https://online.hbs.edu/blog/post/breaking-down-the-demise-of-toys-r-us.

47. Bakke, David. "The Top 25 Investing Quotes of All Time." Investopedia. Last updated September 3, 2025. Accessed August 24, 2025. https://www.investopedia.com/financial-edge/0511/the-top-17-investing-quotes-of-all-time.aspx.

48. Investopedia. "KPIs: What Are Key Performance Indicators? Types and Examples." Accessed August 24, 2025. https://www.investopedia.com/terms/k/kpi.asp.

49. Blank, Steve. "The Four Steps to the Epiphany: Measuring Progress in Startups." *Harvard Business Review*, February 2013. https://hbr.org/2013/02/the-four-steps-to-the-epiphany.

50. Feld, Brad. "Why Customer Acquisition Cost Is the Most Important Metric for Startups." *Forbes*, August 15,

2019. https://www.forbes.com/sites/forbesfinancecoun-cil/2019/08/15/why-customer-acquisition-cost-is-the-most-important-metric-for-startups/.

51. McKinsey & Company. "Growing Faster Than Your Competitors: The Role of Customer Lifetime Value." Accessed August 24, 2025. https://www.mckinsey.com/business-functions/marketing-and-sales/our-insights/growing-faster-than-your-competitors.

52. Patel, Neil. "Understanding Burn Rate: A Critical Metric for Startups." *Entrepreneur*, June 10, 2020. https://www.entrepreneur.com/article/351684.

53. Bain & Company. "Customer Retention: The Key to Startup Success." Accessed August 24, 2025. https://www.bain.com/insights/customer-retention-the-key-to-startup-success/.

54. Reichheld, Fred. "The One Number You Need to Grow." *Harvard Business Review*, December 2003. https://hbr.org/2003/12/the-one-number-you-need-to-grow.

55. Cutler, Kim-Mai. "Why Active Users Are the Lifeblood of Startups." TechCrunch, March 12, 2018. https://techcrunch.com/2018/03/12/why-active-users-are-the-lifeblood-of-startups/.

56. Deloitte. "Startup Success: Key Financial Metrics for Entrepreneurs." Accessed August 24, 2025. https://www.deloitte.com/us/en/insights/industry/technology/startup-financial-metrics.html.

57. Investopedia. "Internal Rate of Return (IRR)." Accessed August 24, 2025. https://www.investopedia.com/terms/i/irr.asp.

58. PitchBook. "MOIC and IRR: Key Metrics in Private Equity." Accessed August 24, 2025. https://pitchbook.com/news/articles/moic-and-irr-key-metrics-in-private-equity.

59. Bain & Company. "Private Equity Value Creation: The Power of Operational Excellence." Accessed August 24, 2025. https://www.bain.com/insights/private-equity-value-creation-global-private-equity-report-2023/.

60. McKinsey & Company. "Value Creation in Private Equity." Accessed August 24, 2025. https://www.mckinsey.com/business-functions/strategy-and-corporate-finance/our-insights/value-creation-in-private-equity.

61. Deloitte. "Private Equity: Driving Value Creation in Portfolio Companies." Accessed August 24, 2025. https://www2.deloitte.com/us/en/insights/industry/financial-services/private-equity-value-creation.html.

62. S&P Global. "Leverage Metrics in Private Equity: A Focus on Debt-to-EBITDA." Accessed August 24, 2025. https://www.spglobal.com/marketintelligence/en/news-insights/research/leverage-metrics-in-private-equity.

63. PwC. "Private Equity: Unlocking Value Through Operational Excellence." Accessed August 24, 2025. https://www.pwc.com/gx/en/services/advisory/deals/private-equity/value-creation.html.

64. EY. "Global Private Equity Exit Report 2023." Accessed August 24, 2025. https://www.ey.com/en_gl/private-equity/exit-strategy.

65. "Internal Rate of Return (IRR)." Accessed August 24, 2025. https://www.investopedia.com/terms/i/irr.asp.

66. CFI Team. "Maximizing Returns: Understanding MOIC in Private Equity." CFI. Accessed November 10, 2025. https://corporatefinanceinstitute.com/resources/wealth-management/moic-private-equity/.

67. Bain & Company. "Private Equity Value Creation: The Power of Operational Excellence." Accessed August 24, 2025. https://www.bain.com/insights/private-equity-value-creation-global-private-equity-report-2023/.

68. McKinsey & Company. "Value Creation in Private Equity." Accessed August 24, 2025. https://www.mckinsey.com/business-functions/strategy-and-corporate-finance/our-insights/value-creation-in-private-equity.

69. Deloitte. "Private Equity: Driving Value Creation in Portfolio Companies." Accessed August 24, 2025. https://www2.deloitte.com/us/en/insights/industry/financial-services/private-equity-value-creation.html.

70. S&P Global. "Leverage Metrics in Private Equity: A Focus on Debt-to-EBITDA." Accessed August 24, 2025. https://www.spglobal.com/marketintelligence/en/news-insights/research/leverage-metrics-in-private-equity.

71. PwC. "Private Equity: Unlocking Value Through Operational Excellence." Accessed August 24, 2025. https://www.pwc.com/gx/en/services/advisory/deals/private-equity/value-creation.html.

72. EY. "Global Private Equity Exit Report 2023." Accessed August 24, 2025. https://www.ey.com/en_gl/private-equity/exit-strategy.

73. IBM. "What Are AI Hallucinations?" Accessed August 24, 2025. https://www.ibm.com/think/topics/ai-hallucinations.

74. Edelman, Rob. "Dunkin' Donuts." Encyclopedia.com, 2002. Accessed October 1, 2025. https://www.encyclopedia.com/history/culture-magazines/dunkin-donuts.

75. The Family Office. "Inside Private Equity: A Case Study of Triumphs and Failures." November 6, 2024. https://thefamilyoffice.ch/inside-private-equity-a-case-study-of-triumphs-and-failures.

76. The Family Office. "Inside Private Equity: A Case Study of Triumphs and Failures." November 6, 2024. https://thefamilyoffice.ch/inside-private-equity-a-case-study-of-triumphs-and-failures.

77. Adams, Susan. "Dunkin' Donuts Takes on the World: Leadership Lessons from the CEO." *Forbes*, October 1, 2013. https://www.forbes.com/sites/susanadams/2013/10/01/dunkin-donuts-takes-on-the-world-leadership-lessons-from-the-ceo/.

78. Chief Executive. "Former Dunkin' CEO Nigel Travis: 'Challenge Everything.'" *Chief Executive*. Accessed August 24, 2025. https://chiefexecutive.net/former-dunkin-ceo-nigel-travis-challenge-everything/.

79. Abercrombie & Fitch Co. "Nigel Travis." Abercrombie & Fitch Co. https://corporate.abercrombie.com/blog/leadership/nigel-travis/.

80. Adams, Susan. "Dunkin' Donuts Takes on the World: Leadership Lessons from the CEO." *Forbes*, October 1, 2013. https://www.forbes.com/sites/susanadams/2013/10/01/

dunkin-donuts-takes-on-the-world-leadership-lessons-from-the-ceo/.

81. Chamorro-Premuzic, Tomas, Seymour Adler, and Robert B. Kaiser. "What Science Says About Identifying High-Potential Employees." *Harvard Business Review*, October 3, 2017. https://hbr.org/2017/10/what-science-says-about-identifying-high-potential-employees.

82. Rampton, Deanna. "The Story of Building Tesla, with Marc Tarpenning of Tesla and Shehnaz Daver of GV." Startup Grind. September 25, 2017. https://www.startupgrind.com/blog/the-story-of-building-tesla-with-marc-tarpenning-of-tesla-and-shernaz-daver-of-gv/.

83. Java, Kim, host. "Tesla's Forgotten Founder Speaks Out – Exclusive w/ Martin Eberhard." August 28, 2024. YouTube. https://www.youtube.com/watch?v=88KHfX_kPIY.

84. Java, Kim, host. "Tesla's Forgotten Founder Speaks Out – Exclusive w/ Martin Eberhard." August 28, 2024. YouTube. https://www.youtube.com/watch?v=88KHfX_kPIY.

85. Schreiber, Barbara A. "Martin Eberhard and Marc Tarpenning." Britannica. May 16, 2024. Accessed September 28, 2024. https://www.britannica.com/money/Martin-Eberhard-and-Marc-Tarpenning.

86. Java, Kim, host. "Tesla's Forgotten Founder Speaks Out – Exclusive w/ Martin Eberhard." August 28, 2024. YouTube. https://www.youtube.com/watch?v=88KHfX_kPIY.

87. Moskowitz, Dan. "The 10 Richest People in the World." Investopedia, November 1, 2025. https://www.investopedia.com/articles/investing/012715/5-richest-people-world.asp.

88. Java, Kim, host. "Tesla's Forgotten Founder Speaks Out – Exclusive w/ Martin Eberhard." August 28, 2024. YouTube. https://www.youtube.com/watch?v=88KHfX_kPIY.

89. Java, Kim, host. "Tesla's Forgotten Founder Speaks Out – Exclusive w/ Martin Eberhard." August 28, 2024. YouTube. https://www.youtube.com/watch?v=88KHfX_kPIY.

90. Apex Business Advisors. "Case Study 76: Veterinary Mini Roll-Up." Accessed November 10, 2025. https://www.kcapex.com/case-study-76-veterinary-mini-roll-up/.

91. Apex Business Advisors. "Case Study 76: Veterinary Mini Roll-Up." Accessed November 10, 2025. https://www.kcapex.com/case-study-76-veterinary-mini-roll-up/.

92. *Built to Sell*. "A Behind-the-Scenes Look at a Mini Rollup." November 4, 2022. https://builttosell.com/radio/episode-362/.

93. Apex Business Advisors. "Case Study #76: Veterinary Mini Roll-Up." July 24, 2023. https://www.kcapex.com/case-study-76-veterinary-mini-roll-up/.

94. Apex Business Advisors. "Case Study #76: Veterinary Mini Roll-Up." July 24, 2023. https://www.kcapex.com/case-study-76-veterinary-mini-roll-up/.

95. Hoffman, Reid, Ben Casnocha, and Chris Yeh. "Tours of Duty: The New Employer-Employee Compact." *Harvard Business Review*, June 2013. https://hbr.org/2013/06/tours-of-duty-the-new-employer-employee-compact.

96. Hoffman, Reid, Ben Casnocha, and Chris Yeh. "Tours of Duty: The New Employer-Employee Compact." *Harvard*

Business Review, June 2013. https://hbr.org/2013/06/tours-of-duty-the-new-employer-employee-compact.

97. Hoffman, Reid, Ben Casnocha, and Chris Yeh. "Tours of Duty: The New Employer-Employee Compact." *Harvard Business Review*, June 2013. https://hbr.org/2013/06/tours-of-duty-the-new-employer-employee-compact.

98. Kruse, Kevin. "100 Best Quotes on Leadership." *Forbes*, October 16, 2012. https://www.forbes.com/sites/kevinkruse/2012/10/16/quotes-on-leadership/.

99. Chen, James. "Board of Directors: Definition and Role." Investopedia, May 20, 2025.

100. American Investment Council. "ICYMI: WSJ Highlights How Private Equity Transforms Plumbing and HVAC Small Businesses, Boosting Wages and Growth." October 15, 2024. https://www.investmentcouncil.org/icymi-wsj-highlights-how-private-equity-transforms-plumbing-and-hvac-small-businesses-boosting-wages-and-growth/.

101. "Private Equity Is Pouring Money into Skilled-Trade Small Businesses: Excerpts from *The Wall Street Journal*." Multi-Briefs, October 2024. https://multibriefs.com/briefs/cema/Privateequity.pdf. Originally published as Te-Ping Chen, "America's New Millionaire Class: Plumbers and HVAC Entrepreneurs," *Wall Street Journal*, October 12, 2024.

102. Rite Way Heating, Cooling & Plumbing. "About Rite Way." Accessed November 5, 2025. https://ritewayac.com/about-riteway/.

103. "Redwood Services Announces Strategic Partnership with Rite Way." HVAC & Refrigeration Insider Online, March 29,

2021. https://hvacinsider.com/redwood-services-announces-strategic-partnership-with-rite-way/.

104. "Redwood Services Announces Strategic Partnership with Rite Way." HVAC & Refrigeration Insider Online, March 29, 2021. https://hvacinsider.com/redwood-services-announces-strategic-partnership-with-rite-way/.

105. "Redwood Services Announces Strategic Partnership with Rite Way." HVAC & Refrigeration Insider Online, March 29, 2021. https://hvacinsider.com/redwood-services-announces-strategic-partnership-with-rite-way/.

106. Southern New Hampshire University. "50 Personal Growth Quotes to Inspire Your Journey." SNHU. August 8, 2022. https://www.snhu.edu/about-us/newsroom/education/personal-growth-quotes.

107. Goodreads. "Aesop Quotes." Accessed November 10, 2025. https://www.goodreads.com/quotes/872676-in-union-there-is-strength.

108. PetSmart. "Our Story." PetSmart Corporate. Accessed August 28, 2025. https://www.petsmartcorporate.com/our-story/.

109. BC Partners. "PetSmart – Chewy." BC Partners. Accessed August 28, 2025. https://www.bcpartners.com/portfolio/petsmart-chewy.

110. BC Partners. "PetSmart – Chewy." BC Partners. Accessed August 28, 2025. https://www.bcpartners.com/portfolio/petsmart-chewy.

111. Del Rey, Jason. "PetSmart Buys Chewy." CNBC, April 18, 2017. https://www.cnbc.com/2017/04/18/petsmart-buys-chewy.html.

112. Knutson, Ryan, and Jessica Mendoza, hosts. *The Journal.* "How PetSmart Solved Its Chewy Problem (featuring Miriam Gottfried)." *Wall Street Journal*, December 3, 2019. https://www.wsj.com/podcasts/the-journal/how-petsmart-solved-its-chewy-problem/3cb86a84-133d-4a21-b19d-7981e90d1508.

113. Axios. "Behind PetSmart's $3.3 Billion Chewy Acquisition." December 15, 2017. https://www.axios.com/2017/12/15/behind-petsmarts-33-billion-chewy-acquisition-1513301711.

114. Knutson, Ryan, and Jessica Mendoza, hosts. *The Journal.* "How PetSmart Solved Its Chewy Problem (featuring Miriam Gottfried)." *Wall Street Journal*, December 3, 2019. https://www.wsj.com/podcasts/the-journal/how-petsmart-solved-its-chewy-problem/3cb86a84-133d-4a21-b19d-7981e90d1508.

115. Knutson, Ryan, and Jessica Mendoza, hosts. *The Journal.* "How PetSmart Solved Its Chewy Problem (featuring Miriam Gottfried)." *Wall Street Journal*, December 3, 2019. https://www.wsj.com/podcasts/the-journal/how-petsmart-solved-its-chewy-problem/3cb86a84-133d-4a21-b19d-7981e90d1508.

116. Knutson, Ryan, and Jessica Mendoza, hosts. *The Journal.* "How PetSmart Solved Its Chewy Problem (featuring Miriam Gottfried)." *Wall Street Journal*, December 3, 2019. https://www.wsj.com/podcasts/the-journal/how-petsmart-solved-its-chewy-problem/3cb86a84-133d-4a21-b19d-7981e90d1508.

117. Vien, Courtney. "The Astonishing Growth of PE-Backed CPA Firms." CFO Brew, October 18,

2024. https://www.cfobrew.com/stories/2024/10/18/
the-astonishing-growth-of-pe-backed-cpa-firms/.

118. Vien, Courtney. "The Astonishing Growth of
PE-Backed CPA Firms." CFO Brew, October 18,
2024. https://www.cfobrew.com/stories/2024/10/18/
the-astonishing-growth-of-pe-backed-cpa-firms/.

119. Vien, Courtney. "The Astonishing Growth of
PE-Backed CPA Firms." CFO Brew, October 18,
2024. https://www.cfobrew.com/stories/2024/10/18/
the-astonishing-growth-of-pe-backed-cpa-firms/.

120. Greenwell, Megan. "How Private Equity Killed the American
Dream." *WIRED*, June 17, 2025. https://www.wired.com/
story/private-equity-bad-company-megan-greenwell/.

121. Univio. "10 Digital Transformation Challenges to
Overcome." February 6, 2024. https://www.univio.com/
insights/10-digital-transformation-challenges-to-overcome.

122. Barber, Felix, and Michael Goold. "The Strategic Secret of
Private Equity." *Harvard Business Review*, September 2007.
https://hbr.org/2007/09/the-strategic-secret-of-private-equity.

123. Salesforce SMB Team. "40 Inspiring Quotes About Business
Growth — and Tips for Success." Salesforce, September 19,
2025. Accessed October 24, 2025. https://www.salesforce.
com/blog/inspirational-business-quotes/.

124. Java, Kim, host. "Tesla's Forgotten Founder Speaks Out —
Exclusive w/ Martin Eberhard." August 28, 2024. YouTube.
https://www.youtube.com/watch?v=88KHfX_kPIY.

125. Eberhard, Martin, and Marc Tarpenning. "Tesla Founders Martin Eberhard and Marc Tarpenning Talk About the Early Days and Bringing on Elon Musk." Interview by Lora Kolodny. CNBC, February 6, 2021. https://www.cnbc.com/2021/02/06/tesla-founders-martin-eberhard-marc-tarpenning-on-elon-musk.html.

126. Hayes, Adam. "Tesla: The True Untold Story." Investopedia, September 2025. https://www.investopedia.com/articles/personal-finance/061915/story-behind-teslas-success.asp.

127. Crunchbase. "Martin Eberhard – Investor Timeline." Crunchbase. Accessed October 31, 2025. https://www.crunchbase.com/person/martin-eberhard/person_overview_investor/timeline.

128. Salesforce SMB Team. "40 Inspiring Quotes About Business Growth — and Tips for Success." Salesforce, September 19, 2025. https://www.salesforce.com/blog/inspirational-business-quotes/.

129. Practice Transitions Group. "What Is Rolling Equity? Definition and Tips for Successful Negotiations." Practice Transitions Group. Accessed October 30, 2025. https://practicetransitionsgroup.com/blog/what-is-rolling-equity-definition-and-tips-for-successful-negotiations/.

130. Wiessner, Daniel. "Trump Administration Drops Defense of Ban on Employee 'Noncompete' Agreements." Reuters, September 5, 2025. https://www.reuters.com/legal/litigation/trump-administration-drops-defense-ban-employee-noncompete-agreements-2025-09-06/.

131. Pimlico Plumbers Ltd. v. Smith [2018] UKSC 29. Accessed November 10, 2025. https://supremecourt.uk/uploads/uksc_2017_0053_press_summary_fc5d49d452.pdf.

132. Shopee Singapore Pte. Ltd. v. Lim Teck Yong. [2024] SGHC 29. https://www.elitigation.sg/gd/gd/2024_SGHC_29/pdf.

133. Twenty Four Motors CC t/a Ford Ermelo v. Andries Johannes Jacobus Venter and Others [2024] ZALCJHB 33. https://www.saflii.org/za/cases/ZALCJHB/2024/33.pdf.

134. Sadan and Another v. Workforce Staffing (Pty) Ltd. [2023] ZALAC 14. August 17, 2023. Accessed November 10, 2025. http://www.saflii.org/za/cases/ZALAC/2023/14.html.

135. Fitzpatrick, Maria D., and Timothy J. Moore. "The Mortality Effects of Retirement: Evidence from Social Security Eligibility at Age 62." *Journal of Public Economics* 157 (January 2018): 121–37. https://doi.org/10.1016/j.jpubeco.2017.12.001.

136. Goodreads. "Quotes Tagged 'Beginnings and Endings.'" Goodreads. Accessed October 25, 2025. https://www.goodreads.com/quotes/tag/beginnings-and-endings/.

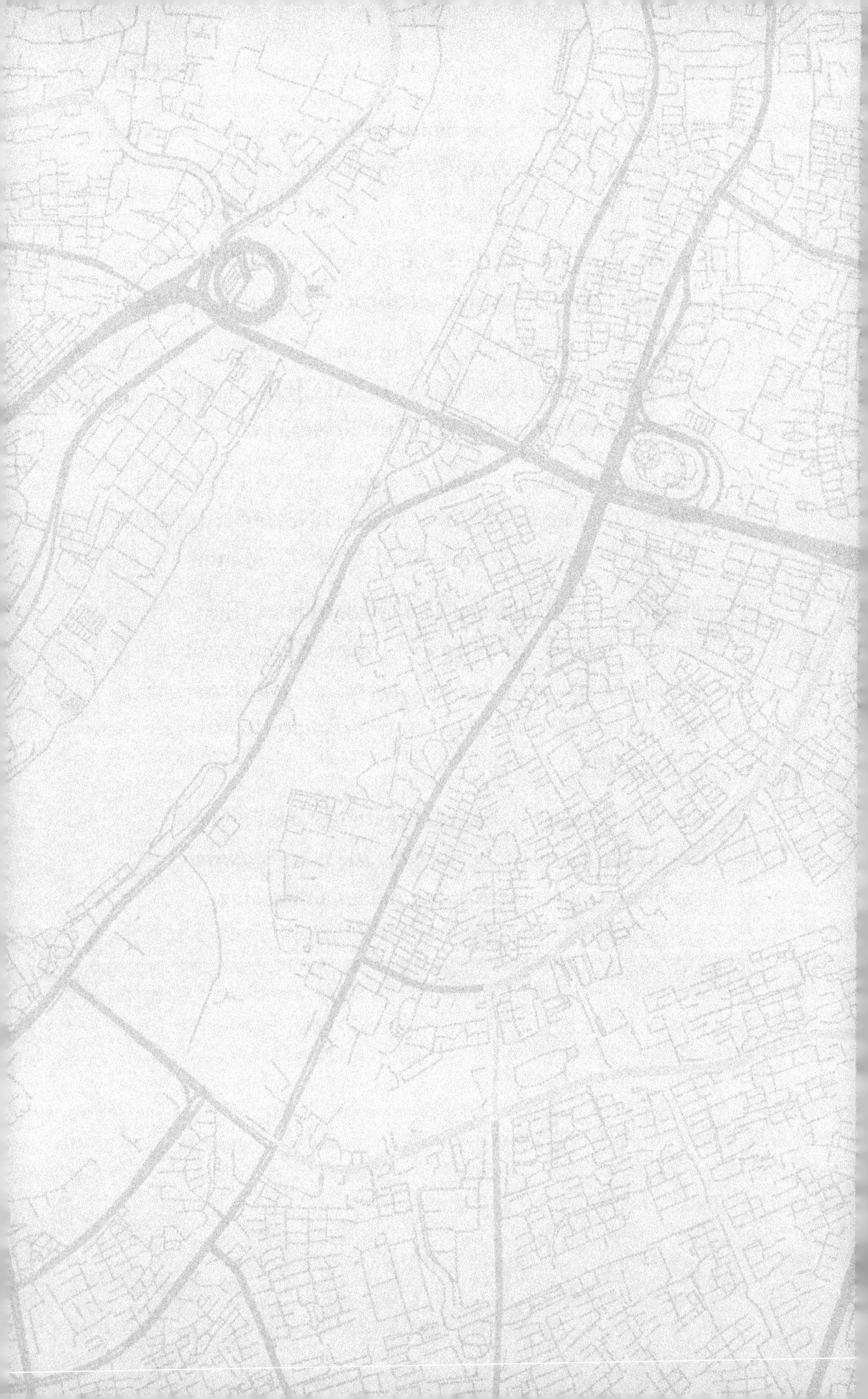

Glossary

Burn rate

How fast a business utilizes its cash.

Business-to-business model

An approach by which a business transacts with another business.

Business-to-consumer model

An approach by which a business transacts with a consumer.

Cash flow metrics

KPIs utilized to gauge the amount, timing, and predictability of a company's cash inflows and outflows.

Customer relationship management

A software system for managing a company's customers throughout the business relationship.

Customer acquisition cost

A KPI that measures the cost of acquiring a new customer.

Customer lifetime value

The total revenue a business projects to reasonably earn from one individual customer.

Customer retention rate

A KPI that measures the percentage of customers a company continues to have over a given period, excluding customers acquired in that same period.

Daily active users

The number of users who engage with a given company over twenty-four hours.

Deal team

A small group of team members that a management team works with. It usually includes an associate, a VP, the president, and a deal lead (partner, managing director, or principle). This team may also include an operating partner. This is the team within the PE firm that has the overall responsibility for a particular investment.

Earnings before interest, taxes, depreciation and amortization (EBITDA)

A KPI that measures a business's operating efficiency by taking into account its cash-generating potential from core business operations and excluding the effects of financing decisions, accounting methods, or tax environments.

Enterprise resource planning

A type of software system used to manage core operational business processes.

Enterprise value

A KPI used to measure the total economic value of a company.

Exit multiples

A KPI used to calculate the anticipated value of a company at the time of its sale.

Free cash flow

A KPI that measures the cash a business yields from its operations after factoring in the money utilized on capital expenditures.

Gross margin

A KPI measuring the finances retained after deducting the cost of goods sold.

Heating, ventilation, and air conditioning

A group of technologies designed to control the indoor climate and air quality in various spaces, including resident, commercial, and mobile.

Indication of interest

A nonbinding document from one business entity to another, expressing interest in a potential business deal.

Internal rate of return

A KPI utilized to gauge the earnings potential of an investment.

Key performance indicator

A financial metric that is utilized to measure progress toward specific criteria and objectives.

Letter of intent

An exclusive agreement of both parties to close the agreement.

Leverage ratio

A KPI utilized to assess the rate at which a business obtains debt to finance its operations and assets.

Monthly active users

The number of users that engage with a given company over thirty days.

Multiple on invested capital

A KPI that measures the overall profit on an investment proportional to the amount of capital originally invested, without considering the value of money over time.

Net promoter scale

A KPI utilized to assess customer loyalty and satisfaction.

Operator

The founder, entrepreneur, or CEO who runs the business.

Operating partner

An individual from the PE firm or representing it in the relationship with the acquired business.

Platform company/platform operator

The company acquiring other companies.

Portfolio company operational metrics

The KPIs typically used by investors for calculating the operational performance of the business they invested in.

Revenue growth

A KPI, typically expressed as a percentage, utilized to measure the rise in a business's sales or revenue over a given period.